The Slavery of Death

The Slavery of Death

RICHARD BECK

CASCADE *Books* · Eugene, Oregon

THE SLAVERY OF DEATH

Cascade Books
An Imprint of Wipf and Stock Publishers
199 W. 8th Ave., Suite 3
Eugene, OR 97401

www.wipfandstock.com

ISBN 13: 978-1-62032-777-7

Cataloguing-in-Publication Data

Beck, Richard Allen, 1967–

    The slavery of death / Richard Beck.

    xiv + 134 p. ; 23 cm. Includes bibliographical references.

    ISBN 13: 978-1-62032-777-7

    1. Death. I. Title.

BD444 .B435 2014

Manufactured in the U.S.A.

For Mom and Dad

Since the children have flesh and blood, he too shared in their humanity so that by his death he might break the power of him who holds the power of death—that is, the devil—and free those who all their lives were held in slavery by their fear of death.

—Hebrews 2:14–15

The way of Jesus is the way of self-expenditure.

—Arthur McGill

Look at your poverty
welcome it
cherish it
don't be afraid
share your death
because thus you will share your love and your life.

—Jean Vanier

Contents

Prelude

"The Sting of Death"

1.

"The sting of death is sin."

So wrote the Apostle Paul in the first letter to the Corinthians.[1] It's a curious formulation if you ponder it, particularly if you come from a Protestant tradition. As Protestants we tend to think that sin is our primary predicament, the reason Jesus Christ died at Golgotha—his death an atoning sacrifice for our sins. But in his words to the Corinthians Paul seems to suggest that sin is a *consequence* of death. If so, death might be our deeper, more significant problem. Sin might be less the *disease* than a *symptom*. Death, in this view, is the cause of sin.

This is a peculiar reversal for many Protestants who have tended to think that death is the consequence of sin. It's sin that causes death, not the other way around. The impulse here is less "the sting of death is sin" than the refrain from Romans 6:23—"The wages of sin is death." And such an understanding is supported by the story in Genesis 3 where, after the primal sin, Adam and Eve are expelled from Eden and separated from the Tree of Life. Romans 5:12: "Therefore, just as sin entered the world through one man, and death through sin, and in this way death came to all people, because all sinned." The sin of Adam and Eve, a sin we recapitulate, brings death into the world—both physical death (mortality) and spiritual death (separation from God).

1. 1 Cor 15:56 NIV.

And yet, there are many passages within the New Testament that place death at the center of the human predicament. For example, it is death, rather than sin, that is considered to be the "last enemy" (1 Cor 15:24–25). In the book of Revelation the last thing to be thrown into the Lake of Fire is death and Hades. And at the end of Romans 7, Paul's long discussion of his experience in wrestling with sin, he concludes with a peculiar cry: "What a wretched man I am! Who will rescue me from this body that is subject to death?" The root of Paul's "sin problem" seems to be that he has, just like the rest of us, a body that is "subject to death."

Another facet of this perspective worth noting is how the Bible describes the activity of the devil. Throughout the New Testament sin, death, and the devil are at times described as almost interchangeable forces, three facets of an ontological unity—a sort of unholy Trinity. Consequently, if we are to have a full biblical understanding concerning the work of Jesus—the work he accomplished in his life, death, and resurrection—we must pay attention to texts like 1 John 3:8: "The reason the Son of God appeared was to destroy the devil's work." What is this "work of the devil"? And how was it destroyed? Most Protestants tend to reduce the role of Satan to that of tempter, and undeniably that is a part of the picture. But the New Testament also describes Satan as holding the power of death. As it says in Hebrews 2:14, the death of Jesus was intended to "destroy him who holds the power of death—that is, the devil." This victory over the devil is reaffirmed in the opening vision of Revelation where the Resurrected Lord is declared to be holding "the keys of death and Hades." Death, once under the power of Satan, is now under the power of Christ.

While this focus on the devil might seem strange to many modern Christians, particularly liberal Christians, this material in the New Testament continues to highlight the centrality of death in the human predicament. Death is seen as "the power of the devil" in our lives. And one reason—perhaps even the primary reason—for Christ's death on the cross was to rob the devil of this power. The reason Christ appeared was to free those who, in the words of Hebrews 2:15, "were all their lives enslaved to the fear of death."

2.

This book will work with a reversal of the traditional Protestant understanding regarding the causal association between sin and death. The traditional understanding:

Protestant Formulation:

Sin causes Death.
Biblical articulation: "The wages of sin is death" (Rom 6:23).

The frame we will be focusing on reverses this association. This is an understanding that has been largely marginalized within the Protestant tradition. However, as we will see, this understanding was common in the first centuries of the church and it continues to inform the Eastern Orthodox church:

Orthodox Formulation:

Death causes Sin.
Biblical articulation: "The sting of death is sin" (1 Cor 15:56).

Looking at both formulations, what we find is a complex causal tangle, even before we throw the devil into the mix. So to be clear, the perspective of this book, which emphasizes the moral impact of death upon our lives, isn't an attempt to replace the Protestant framing. Rather, the goal is to point out how the Protestant tradition, in placing the primary emphasis upon sin, has ignored a wealth of biblical material regarding the nature of sin and salvation. The Bible presents us with a dense and complex causal matrix in which sin, death, and the devil all mutually interact. Consequently, an exclusive focus on sin tends to oversimplify the dynamics of our moral struggles. I argue that a fuller analysis is critical as it will present us with a clearer picture of Christian virtue—love in particular. By exposing the dynamics of "the devil's work" in our lives, works produced by a "slavery to the fear of death," we will be better positioned to resist the satanic influences in our lives, better equipped to do battle with the principalities and powers of darkness, and better able to love as Christ loved us.

3.

As noted above, while treating death as our primary predicament may seem strange to some, this perspective is the norm within the Eastern Orthodox tradition. Thus much of this book (particularly Part 1) will mine the riches of the Orthodox tradition, which brings us to a question: If a great deal of the theological material included can be found within the Orthodox tradition, why should one choose to read a book written by a Protestant psychologist?

Excellent question.

The answer goes back to the biblical notion of Satan wielding "the power of death." What sort of power is this? How exactly does death have *power*, a *moral* power, over us? A text that unpacks this dynamic—the moral power of death—is Hebrews 2:14–15:

> Since the children have flesh and blood, he too shared in their humanity so that by his death he might break the power of him who holds the power of death—that is, the devil—and free those who all their lives were held in slavery by their fear of death.

The power of death that the devil wields is characterized here as a *slavery to the fear of death*. It is not death per se that gives the devil power. It is, rather, the *fear* of death. It is this fear that creates the satanic influence, a fear that tempts us into sinful practices and lifestyles, a fear that keeps us demonically "possessed" in our idolatrous service to the principalities and powers.

Salvation, then, involves liberation from this fear. Salvation is emancipation for those who have been enslaved all of their lives by the fear of death. Salvation is a deliverance that sets us free from this power of the devil.

What might be the sign of this liberation? In the biblical imagination the antithesis of fear is love. Freedom from the fear of death makes love possible. As it says in 1 John 4:18, "There is no fear in love. But perfect love drives out fear . . ." Where fear is a symptom of death, love becomes a sign of resurrection: "Anyone who does not love remains in death" (1 John 3:14). Where we find fear and death on one side, we find love and resurrection on the other.

Here, then, is where psychology fits into the picture. While there is a great deal of theological literature to consult regarding Orthodox or *Christus Victor* theology, there is precious little work from theologians on how death anxiety produces "the works of the devil." There is, however, a great deal of *psychological* literature—both empirical and theoretical—that has connected death anxiety with a variety of unhealthy outcomes—psychological, social, and moral. This psychological research holds great potential for unpacking what the Bible describes as "slavery to the fear of death." This psychological research also has something interesting to say about why perfect love must "cast out fear."

To date, however, no one has brought this psychological research into conversation with theology. I hope this book will help start that conversation. So while it may seem strange to find a psychologist writing about Orthodox theology, the ultimate goal of this book is to understand what "slavery to the fear of death" might look like, psychologically speaking, and to explore how perfect love must involve a liberation from this fear.

And since this book is about the relationship between fear and love, a theologically minded psychologist might not be such a bad guide after all.

4.

This book, then, is a prolonged meditation on the role of death anxiety in producing "the devil's works." The book brings modern psychological science into conversation with Orthodox theology to illuminate what the writer of Hebrews describes as "slavery to the fear of death." Phrased positively, the book is a psychological and theological analysis of "perfect love" and why it must "cast out fear."

As we'll come to see in the chapters that follow, slavery to the fear of death affects every facet of the human experience, even the most mundane and workaday. This book is written in the hope that if the dynamics of this slavery are exposed and the deep roots of our sinful practices brought into the light, we might be better able to "cast out fear" in the name of love. But what makes this so hard, as we will come to see, is that our slavery to the fear of death is often so deep, hidden, and repressed that at times it can be impossible to detect our bondage. Then again, this predicament isn't all that surprising. As the Bible warns, the devil often comes to us disguised as an angel of light.

5.

An overview of the book:

Part 1 provides a brief and selective theological summary of Orthodox theology that highlights the role of death as the cause of sin and the "works of the devil." The goal of Part 1 is to help those unfamiliar with this approach, particularly Protestants, to imagine the reversal we have discussed above, seeing death as our central and defining predicament.

After laying a theological foundation in Part 1, we'll turn to psychology in Part 2 and unpack Part 1's content in light of modern psychological research. In other words, Part 2 will describe the "slavery to the fear of death" and its role in producing "the devil's works" from a psychological perspective, attempting to translate theology into something psychologically recognizable. *How, exactly, might I be enslaved to the fear of death in my day-to-day experiences and interactions with others? And how might this slavery cause me to behave sinfully?* With a concrete psychological picture in hand we'll be better positioned to understand what love involves from within the Christian experience. Part 3, then, will focus on love, concluding with a positive discussion of how love leads to emancipation from the fear of death and how that liberation might be accomplished.

PART 1

"The Last Enemy"

Chapter 1

———— ∞∞∞ ————

Ancestral Sin

1.

The central contention of this book is that death, not sin, is the primary predicament of the human condition. Death is the cause of sin. More properly, the fear of death produces most of the sin in our lives.

The most obvious objection to this line of argument is an appeal to the sequence recounted in Genesis 3, a sequence Paul later echoes in Romans 5:12. As the Genesis text describes, Adam and Eve's original disobedience effected a separation from the Tree of Life, and that first sin is what introduced both death and mortality into the world. Clearly, then, sin brings about death and not the other way around. And doesn't Paul affirm that "the wages of sin is death"?

No doubt that *in the Genesis story* a primal disobedience precedes the introduction of death into the world. In that account, sin comes first and results in death—this much seems clear. But the issue we must consider as we go forward is this: how much of our current situation can be modeled on the story of the primal sin? To cut to the chase, we're not in Eden anymore. Unlike Adam and Eve, we are *born into a mortal state*, subject to death from the moment of conception. Before our moral lives begin—before we sin— we are born into a death-saturated existence. Unlike Adam and Eve, death predates us. We live in a very different sort of world than the one described in Genesis 1–2.

In short, the issue going forward, from a biblical perspective, is less about what happened at the *start* of the story than about *the world created by that story*. In Genesis sin might have predated death for Adam and Eve. But in our experience death predates our sin or, at the very least, any moral choices we make. And if death *predates* our sin, might death be implicated in *causing* our sin? Might sin be the *sting*—the poisonous outcome—of death?

2.

We might, then, want to pause and reconsider what exactly we inherited from Adam and Eve in the Genesis story and how that inheritance affects us—morally, spiritually, psychologically, socially, physically, and ecologically. Our particular focus will be on how this inheritance helps us understand the relationship between sin and death.

In Western Christianity this inheritance has generally been understood to be what is called "original sin." Adam and Eve passed on moral brokenness and incapacity, and thus humanity, in this view, is intrinsically sinful. Those who hold to this belief view sin as a congenital moral and spiritual defect that is passed down to us from Adam and Eve, affecting and infecting every living person.[1] In many ways the doctrine of original sin preserves and recapitulates the primal ordering of sin and death in the biography of every person. Since each of us is "born in sin," sin remains the primary predicament, the prime mover and original cause, just as it was with Adam and Eve. And just like Adam and Eve this sinful nature leads us to sin, which then introduces death—both spiritual and physical—into each of our personal biographies. We retrace the story of Genesis 3—sin is our central problem, the causal agent that brings death into our worlds.

---

1. Just how original sin is genetically or psychologically transmitted is unclear. In an effort to link theological notions of original sin with biological and psychological views of human persons, some have suggested that the "moral stain" of original sin might name our Darwinian instincts for survival and self-preservation. I think this move falters when it is pointed out that survival instincts are driven by mortality, survival and death fears. This again makes death the causal agent behind sin. While I agree, as I will argue in this book, that survival fears are at the root of human sinfulness, I don't think this move supports Western views of original sin. This move does, however, sit well with Orthodox views of ancestral sin, the topic of this chapter. In short, I think Orthodox theology and its view of ancestral sin is better positioned than Western theology and its notion of original sin to converse with the biological and social sciences. Those who want to build bridges between theology and science might want to take note of this.

3.

The doctrine of original sin is well known, but that's not to say that it is un-contested in Western Christianity. Still, for our purposes even those whose traditions reject the doctrine retain the basic sin/death sequence. That is, they believe that even if infants are born innocent they will eventually reach an "age of accountability" and experience the inevitable first sin and fall from grace, which produces spiritual and physical death. Sin might not be intrinsic but it's *inevitable*. And death always follows as the consequence.

Yet, despite its ubiquity in the West, we need not take original sin as the authoritative view on what exactly we have inherited from Adam and Eve. Specifically, the Eastern Orthodox tradition does not endorse the West-ern notion of original sin, but rather espouses a view called ancestral sin. Where original sin sees sin as producing death, ancestral sin tends to flip this sequence and place most of the emphasis upon the power of death.

4.

Why is there death if a perfect and loving God created the world? According to the Orthodox, the real issue at the heart of Genesis 3—the biblical story of "the Fall"—is not focused on establishing a causal model regarding the sin/death relationship and how we inherit a moral stain from our ancestors, but is mostly concerned about *the etiology of death* and who is to blame for introducing death into the world. In other words, the Eastern Orthodox tradition understands Genesis 3 to be more about *theodicy* (a story about where death came from) than *soteriology* (a story about where sin came from).

The answer given in Genesis 3 regarding the origins of death is that death wasn't a part of God's divine plan. Death wasn't created by God. Con-sider the bald assertion in the deuterocanonical book of Wisdom: "God did not make death" (Wis 1:13 NRSV). If that's the case then how did death get here? Wisdom points to two different causes. The first is the devil:

> For God created us for incorruption, and made us in the image
> of his own eternity, but through the devil's envy death entered
> the world. . . . (Wisdom 2:23–24a NRSV)

This explanation jibes well with Genesis 3. In the garden the serpent pre-dates death and human sin and is there at the start, tempting Eve into eating the apple, which ultimately leads to the introduction of death into the world.

And yet, the devil needed willing participants. Thus, Wisdom also puts blame upon humanity:

> Do not invite death by the error of your life,
> or bring on destruction by the works of your hands;
> because God did not make death,
> and does not delight in the death of the living.
> For he created all things so that they might exist;
> the generative forces of the world are wholesome,
> and there is no destructive poison in them,
> and the dominion of Hades is not on earth.
> For righteousness is immortal.
> But the ungodly by their words and deeds summoned death;
> considering him a friend, they pined away and made a covenant
> with him . . . (Wis 1:12–16a, NRSV)

In addition to the "envy of the devil" introducing death into the world, the words and deeds of the ungodly "summoned" death. We can understand this as being both a historical account and an ongoing reality: Adam and Eve summoned death and we, in word and deed, recapitulate their sin and thus continue to summon death. We live life controlled by a "covenant with death." In the language of Hebrews 2:15, we are "slaves to the fear of death."

We should note that Wisdom, as a deuterocanonical book, informs the imaginations of the Orthodox and Catholic traditions but is relatively unknown to many Protestants. And what we find in Wisdom, returning to Genesis 3, is less a description of a "fall from moral perfection" than a story about the etiology of death. To be sure, human disobedience is a part of this story. But the main impulse of the story, given how the Orthodox follow the framing given in texts like those in Wisdom, is less about how the world became infected by sin than how it became infected by death. And looking at the Genesis 3 narrative, we see that the root cause of death isn't sin, as the devil/serpent actually predates sin. It's the "envy of the devil" that introduces sin and death into the world.

These understandings go a fair way in providing context for many New Testament texts, illuminating why Jesus came to "undo the works of the devil" (1 John 3:8) and to "break the power of him who holds the power of death—that is, the devil" (Heb 2:14). These texts explain why death is the "last enemy" of Christ, as well as why the book of Revelation is keen to show the resurrected Jesus as holding the keys of death.

In all this, we see how the Eastern Orthodox tradition offers a different understanding regarding the events in Genesis 3. Specifically, we see that the primary purpose of Genesis 3 might be to provide a story about the origins of death rather than the origins of sin. Phrased another way, Genesis 3 might be less interested in explaining why humans are "depraved" than it is in explaining why we die. We do inherit a predicament from the Primal Couple, but what we inherit isn't a moral stain. Rather, we inherit the *world* they have left us. We are exiles from Eden. The world around us is not as God intended it. Death exists, but this was not God's plan. We were created for incorruption but find ourselves to be, in the words of Paul (Romans 7), possessors of bodies that are "subject to death," a subjugation that brings about moral "wretchedness."

And so the simple take-home point of Genesis 3 is this: our bodies, and all of the created order, are infected with death and subject to death. The story, instead of emphasizing a congenital moral defect, tries to explain the view out of our present windows. "Look around you," the text encourages. "This isn't Eden. Death is here."

So death wasn't a part of God's plan for us. But now that death reigns, brought into creation by the devil and human disobedience, we find ourselves enslaved to the fear of death. And so we, along with all of creation, cry out for rescue.

> We know that the whole creation has been groaning as in the pains of childbirth right up to the present time. Not only so, but we ourselves, who have the firstfruits of the Spirit, groan inwardly as we wait eagerly for our adoption to sonship, the redemption of our bodies. (Rom 8:22–23)

5.

If Genesis 3 is a story about the etiology of death, making death the primary predicament in our post-Eden condition, how does death relate to human sinfulness? Again, as we've seen in the account above, sin, death, and the devil are deeply intertwined. So the issue here isn't to displace the importance or role of sin in bringing about death, but to embed our understandings of human moral failure within a richer theological matrix. In the matrix used by the Orthodox, what we have inherited from Adam and Eve is less *a moral stain* than *the mortal condition*, a world and a body infected with death. Rather than original sin—a moral depravity and incapacity passed on from generation to generation—we have a death-infected world created by a primal act of disobedience. Thus the Orthodox don't speak of *original* sin but of an *ancestral* sin, a primal event where death was introduced into the world. The condition we inherit from Adam and Eve is less *moral* than *mortal*.

This isn't to say that the Orthodox marginalize the power and ubiquity of sin in our lives. But the frame here has shifted in an interesting way. As mortal creatures, separated from God's vivifying Spirit, humans are fearful and survival-driven animals, easily drawn into sinful and selfish practices. Because we are mortal and driven by self-preservation, our survival instincts make us tragically vulnerable to death anxiety—the desire to preserve our own existence above all else and at all costs. And as we've seen in Hebrews 2:14–15, Satan uses this fear to enslave us, to keep us rooted in disobedience and continually separated from God. Salvation, in this view, becomes about breaking this *cycle*—the tragic feedback loop of the human condition—in which sin produces death and death makes us vulnerable to sin. Theologian S. Mark Heim summarizes the Orthodox view; removed from Eden, we are

> unnourished by the divine energy, [and] our existence fades into subjection to corruption and death. In such a state, our mortality becomes a source of anxiety. Futile attempts to defend ourselves from it lead us into active sin and estrange us from trust in God. Now sinfulness is more a result of mortality than mortality from sinfulness. To say that humans are "conceived in sin" does not mean that some guilt or evil inclination is passed on to them in the act of their conception, but that what they inherit is a mortal human nature, which became mortal as a result of sin.[2]

6.

In Paul's epistles our animal vulnerability to sin is captured by the Greek word *sarx*, often translated as "flesh." Unfortunately, Paul's use of the term *sarx* in a dizzying array of contexts has led to a great deal of confusion.

Sarx is a key term in Paul's anthropology—it occurs ninety-one times in his letters and twenty-six times in Romans. While *sarx* is generally translated as "flesh," it is also interpreted as "human limitation," "natural limitation," "weakness of the flesh," "the weakness of our natural selves," "the weakness of our human nature," "the weakness of our sinful nature," "sinful nature," "fleshly desires," and "sinful flesh." Consequently, it is hard for readers of English translations to know exactly when and where Paul uses the word *sarx*.

---

2. Heim, *Depth of the Riches*, 68.

This situation is further complicated by the fact that Paul doesn't seem to use *sarx* in a consistent fashion. Attempting to clarify the issue, James Dunn offers a helpful analysis that shows how Paul's use of *sarx* reflects a continuum of meanings. At one end, there are verses in which *sarx* seems to have a benign and neutral meaning, a simple straightforward reference to our physical bodies. Consider Romans 11:14: "in the hope that I may somehow arouse my own people [*sarx*] to envy and save some of them." Here Paul refers to his own "flesh," his biological relationship with the Jewish people. In this instance, nothing hints at the notion of "sinful nature." *Sarx* is simply pointing to bodies, to flesh. Moving away from this neutral meaning, there are passages in which Paul suggests that *sarx* involves limitation, but a limitation without any moral or sinful connotation—for example, Romans 6:19: "I put this in human terms because you are weak in your natural selves [*sarx*]." Here Paul suggests that *sarx* involves a natural limitation, but this "weakness" isn't moral. Rather, it is a cognitive and intellectual limitation, one that makes it hard to *understand* certain things that Paul is trying to communicate. Paul has to work a bit harder to explain spiritual things because his listeners are *sarx*.

Beyond these fairly benign uses of *sarx,* there are times when the term clearly carries a negative moral connotation. Consider the following:

> For when we were controlled by the sinful nature [*sarx*], the sinful passions aroused by the law were at work in our bodies, so that we bore fruit for death. (Rom 7:5)

> The mind of sinful man [*sarx*] is death, but the mind controlled by the Spirit is life and peace; the sinful mind [*sarx*] is hostile to God. It does not submit to God's law, nor can it do so. (Rom 8:6–7)

Here we find *sarx* to be something more sinister, a location where sinful passions are aroused—passions that lead to sin and death. In these cases, *sarx* creates hostility and rebellion toward God.

What can account for these disparate meanings? What did *sarx*—flesh—mean for Paul? According to Dunn, 1 Corinthians 15:35–50 offers a theological clue. In his discussion of the resurrection Paul plainly communicates that our resurrected state will be *bodily* in nature (Paul's word for *body* in this passage is *soma*). Paul is clear that the heavenly existence will have *soma*, embodiment. Each "natural body [*soma*]" will change into a "spiritual body [*soma*]." While *soma*/body will be carried forward in the resurrection, *sarx* will be left behind. As Paul explains in verse 50, "flesh [*sarx*] and blood cannot inherit the kingdom of God, nor does the perishable inherit the imperishable." *Sarx* is here linked with the notion of *perishability*, the fact that our flesh is corruptible and subject to decay and death. We are *mortal*. We don't escape our *bodies* (*soma*) at the resurrection. Rather, our bodies shed *sarx*—their *vulnerability to death*—as the "mortal takes on immortality."

According to Dunn, the association between *sarx* and mortality is what gives *sarx* a consistent and coherent meaning in Paul's writings. Dunn writes,

> [*Sarx* denotes] what we might describe as human mortality. It is the continuum of human mortality, the person characterized and conditioned by human frailty, which gives *sarx* its spectrum of meaning and which provides the link between Paul's different uses of the term.[3]

Sarx is mortal, animal flesh. In some contexts this is a simple and straightforward empirical observation. Crudely, we are animals. We are meat. Flesh. And as mere animals we are subject to animal passions. We are driven, like all animals, by hedonic desires, most of which are meant to insure survival and self-preservation in a Darwinian world.

This understanding of *sarx* fits well with the Orthodox understanding of ancestral sin. Where Western Christianity has tended to interpret *sarx* as a depraved and congenital "sin nature," the Orthodox see *sarx* as *mortality*—our corruptibility and perishability in the face of death. And it's this vulnerability, Paul explains, that makes us susceptible to sin. The idea here is that we are less *wicked* than we are *weak*. As *sarx*—as mortal animals—we are playthings of the devil, who uses the fear of death to push and pull our survival instincts (our fleshly, *sarx*-driven passions) to keep us as "slaves to sin." This explains why Paul, after discussing his struggles with sin at length in Romans 7, goes on to petition, "Who will rescue me from *this body that is subject to death*?" Paul's *weakness* in the face of sin is attributed to his *mortal condition*. Sin here is seen as a symptom of death, the underlying disease.

7.

All this greatly reconfigures how many Western Christians, particularly Protestants, think about sin, original sin, and the "sin nature" we are presumed to have inherited from Adam and Eve. In many ways, the picture we have in hand is much simpler. We are simply mortal creatures. Animals. *Sarx*. Furthermore, this picture jibes nicely with straightforwardly empirical

3. Dunn, *Theology of Paul the Apostle*, 66.

and scientific assessments of the human condition. While there is a lively controversy regarding the metaphysics of original sin and how that sin is transmitted from parents to offspring, there is little debate about the fact that we all die. Nor is there much debate about how our vulnerability to death makes us fearful, paranoid, and suspicious creatures and that these fears promote a host of moral and social ills. As vulnerable, biodegradable creatures in a world of real or potential scarcity, we are prone to act defensively and aggressively toward others who might place our survival at risk. In the Western political tradition perhaps no one has described this situation better than Thomas Hobbes. Consider Mark Lilla's description of our Hobbesian situation, found in his book *The Stillborn God*:

> Natural man, according to Hobbes, is desiring man—which also means he is fearful man. If he finds himself alone in nature he will try to satisfy his desires, will only partially succeed, and will fear losing what he has. But if other human beings are present that fear will be heightened to an almost unbearable degree. Given his awareness of himself as a creature beset by desire— a stream of desire that ends, says Hobbes, only in death—he assumes others are similarly driven. "Whosoever looketh into himself and considereth what he doth," Hobbes writes, "he shall thereby read and know, what are the thoughts and passions of all other men." That means he can think of them only as potential competitors, trying to satisfy desires that may come into conflict with his own . . .
>
> That is why the natural social condition of mankind is war—if not explicit, armed hostilities, then a perpetual state of anxious readiness in preparation for conflict. Even the Bible recognizes this tendency. Hobbes asserts: Cain killed his brother not because of an explicit threat but because he feared losing what he had and was ignorant of God's reasons for favoring Abel. Fear, ignorance, and desire are the basic motivations of all human activity, political and religious. One does not have to assume man is fallen, or evil, or possessed by demons to explain why those motivations produce war. One need only understand how these basic motivations combine in the human mind, both when man is alone and when he is in society.[4]

As we can see, the anthropology given to us by the Orthodox tradition aligns well with these sorts of empirical and sociological assessments of the human condition. Compare Lilla's description above with James 4:1–2a:

---

4. Lilla, *Stillborn God*, 81–82.

> What causes fights and quarrels among you? <u>Don't they come</u>
> <u>from your desires that battle within you?</u> You desire but do not
> have, so you kill. You covet but you cannot get what you want,
> so you quarrel and fight.

The formulation here closely follows Hobbes. Why is there violence in the world? Because of a desire motivated by want, lack, and scarcity—whether it be real, potential, or simply perceived scarcity. "You *desire* but do not *have*, so you *kill.*" That's a neat, tidy, and very Hobbesian formulation. And while this convergence shouldn't be determinative, such connections between theology and the social sciences are of interest for those who want to foster cross-disciplinary conversation.[5]

8.

Again, while these ideas may be new to many Western Christians, they are the norm in the Eastern Orthodox tradition, which weaves everything we have discussed into a rich theological tapestry. In his book *The Ancestral Sin*, Orthodox theologian John Romanides provides an exceptional summary of his tradition's view of the relationship between sin and death. I'd like to share some of his insights to deepen our discussions.

To begin, Romanides contrasts the Western and Orthodox views of sin and salvation. As we've noted, the Orthodox see the Fall as humanity's descent into corruptibility, which then leads to moral weakness and a continued bondage to Satan. This is a death/resurrection view. On the other hand, the West (particularly Protestantism) has tended to work with a sin/wrath matrix. Romanides comments on this contrast:

> In the East, the fall is understood to be a consequence of man's
> own withdrawal from divine life and the resulting weakness and

5. Let me make a comment for those interested in the work of René Girard and who might want to connect Girard's notions of mimetic rivalry with the Hobbesian formulation given here. According to Girard, violence is produced by imitation and desire. Given that humans imitate each other, we often find ourselves desiring the same things. This leads to rivalry, competition, and, eventually, violence. Girard often describes mimetic rivalry as a process of triangulation, with two people desiring (through the imitation of the other) the same object. What I'd like to point out about this is how Girard's model of triangulation is working with a Hobbesian assumption of scarcity— there is only *one* object of desire for *two* people. If there were *two* objects—if there was "enough" or a surplus—there would be no competition or rivalry. At the very least, rivalry should attenuate. This is not necessarily to disagree with Girard's theory, simply the suggestion that his model of rivalry, violence, and scapegoating can complement the Hobbesain formulation given here. Theorists can debate which, anxiety or mimesis, is the more fundamental dynamic.

disease of human nature. Thus, man himself is seen as the cause [of death] through his cooperation with the devil. . . . The Greek Fathers look upon salvation from a biblical perspective and see it as redemption from death and corruptibility and as the healing of human nature which was assaulted by Satan. . . . It is quite the opposite in the West where salvation does not mean, first and foremost, salvation from death and corruptibility but from divine wrath.[6]

Our predicament, then, is *corruptibility* and how our mortal natures make us vulnerable to Satan and moral disobedience. Unpacking the dynamics of this problem, Romanides offers a formulation—at times almost Darwinian in tone—that is very similar to the Hobbesian picture described above. Note also how the fear of death functions as "the power of the devil" that leads us into violent and selfish practices:

Through the power of death and the devil, sin that reigns in men gives rise to fear and anxiety and to the general instinct of self-preservation or survival. Thus, Satan manipulates man's fear and his desire for self-satisfaction, raising up sin in him. . . . Because of death, man must first attend to the necessities of life in order to stay alive. In this struggle, self-interests are unavoidable. Thus, man is unable to live in accordance with his original destiny of unselfish love. This state of subjection under the reign of death is the root of man's weakness in which he becomes entangled in sin at the urging of the demons and by his own consent. Resting in the hands of the devil, the power of the fear of death is the root from which self-aggrandizement, egotism, hatred, envy, and other similar passions spring up. In addition to the fact that man "subjects himself to anything in order to avoid dying," he constantly fears that his life is without meaning. Thus, he strives to demonstrate to himself and to others that it has worth. . . . Fear and anxiety render man an individual.[7]

This passage is a concise summary of the entire argument to this point. As mortal creatures the selfish pursuit of survival and self-preservation becomes our highest good, and these survival fears lead us into all sorts of sinful practices. Almost every unwholesome pursuit of humanity—from hedonism to self-aggrandizement to acquisitiveness to rivalry to violence—can be traced back to these basic survival fears. The fear of death creates the experience of the satanic in our lives. In all this we again note the close and

6. Romanides, *Ancestral Sin*, 35.
7. Ibid., 162–63.

intimate association between sin, death, and the devil. But the links here are not mysterious, mystical, mythical, or metaphysical. The psychology at work here is clear, simple, and widely attested to. In my opinion this is a remarkable convergence between theology and the social sciences, a bridge we hope to exploit to the fullest in Part 2.

Also worth noting is how this seemingly modern and even scientific view reflects, according to the Orthodox, the earliest teachings of the church. For example, Romanides shares a sermon from the patristic father John Chrysostom:

> He who fears death is a slave and subjects himself to everything in order to avoid dying. . . . [But] he who does not fear death is outside the tyranny of the devil. For indeed "man would give skin for skin, and all things for [the sake of] his life," [Job 2:4] and if a man should decide to disregard this, whose slave is he then? He fears no one, is in terror of no one, is higher than everyone, and is freer than everyone. For he who disregards his own life disregards more so all other things. And when the devil finds such a soul, he can accomplish in it none of his works. Tell me, though, what can he threaten? The loss of money or honor? Or exile from one's country? For these are small things to him "who counteth not even his life dear," says blessed Paul [Acts 20:24].
>
> Do you see that in casting out the tyranny of death, He has dissolved the strength of the devil?[8]

As Chrysostom argues, the one who does not fear death is outside the tyranny of the devil. The reason he gives is clear: the fear of death gives the devil moral traction. When we face the threat of loss, want, or lack, we react defensively, even violently. But if the fear of death is absent the devil is stymied. As Chrysostom says, when the devil finds such a soul he can accomplish none of his works in such a person. The devil can find no foothold, no purchase, no leverage in the psyche of one who has no anxiety. The result is clear: "Do you see that in casting out the tyranny of death, [Christ] has dissolved the strength of the devil?"

---

8. Ibid., 168–69. The excerpt is from Homily IV of Chrysostom's Homilies on Hebrews.

Chapter 2

────────── ∞∞∞ ──────────

Christus Victor

1.

The following story is one you are likely familiar with. Let me tell it in a way that might be less familiar to many Christians.

To begin: prompted by his envy, Satan is successful in bringing death into the world (Wis 2:24) by deceiving humanity in the Garden (Gen 3; John 8:44; 2 Cor 11:3). Now wielding death, Satan holds humanity in bondage due to our fear of death (Heb 2:14–15). Under this bondage Satan continues to deceive (2 Cor 4:4), tempt us into sin (2 Cor 11:3), cause spiritual and physical afflictions (Luke 13:15–17; Matt 9:32–37; Mark 5:1–20), thwart the gospel (Matt 13:19), and promote violence (John 8:44). Due to Satan's power, humans are vulnerable and in need of protection (Matt 6:13) since our "enemy the devil prowls around like a roaring lion looking for someone to devour" (1 Pet 5:8).

To set humanity free from this bondage, with all of its moral, social, ecological, psychological, spiritual, and physical afflictions, Christ is born into our world. He comes to "share in [our] humanity so that by his death he might break the power of him who holds the power of death—that is, the devil" (Heb 2:14–15). For "the reason the Son of God appeared was to destroy the devil's work" (1 John 3:8).

Suspecting something about the child of Mary and Joseph, Satan tries to kill Jesus as an infant (Matt 2:13–18; Rev 12:4) but, due to divine intervention, the child escapes. Later, after God publicly identifies Jesus as the

Messiah (Matt 3:13–17), Satan immediately moves to defeat Jesus in a direct confrontation (Matt 4:1–11). Failing in this attempt, Satan leaves Jesus to "wait for an opportune time" (Luke 4:13) to attack again.

For the next three years, Satan and Jesus confront each other in the lives of suffering people as "Jesus went around doing good and healing all who were under the power of the devil" (Acts 10:38). By binding Satan on earth Jesus shows that the Kingdom of God has been inaugurated (Matt 12:22–28). Jesus "drives out the prince of this world" (John 12:28–32), setting free those who were held in bondage to Satan (Luke 13:15–17). The Kingdom continually expands, and Jesus' followers report their own power over Satan; thus the victory seems to be in hand as Jesus sees Satan "falling like lightning from heaven" (Luke 10:17–18).

On the brink of defeat Satan makes his move, entering the heart of Judas to betray Jesus (Luke 22:2–4; John 13:2, 27; John 14:30). Fully aware that this is happening, Jesus goes to Gethsemane to pray and to wait for Judas. In accordance with God's plan, there Jesus is handed over and eventually crucified (Acts 2:23–24). "But God raised this Jesus from the dead, freeing him from the agony of death, because it was impossible for death to keep its hold on him" (Acts 2:25). Being raised from the dead, Jesus "disarmed the powers and authorities and made a public spectacle of them, triumphing over them by the cross" (Col 2:15). Now ascended into heaven, Jesus reigns and will eventually "hand over the kingdom to God the Father after he has destroyed all dominion, authority and power. For he must reign until he has put all his enemies under his feet. The last enemy to be destroyed is death" (1 Cor 15:24–25). When Satan and death are finally defeated and thrown into the Lake of Fire (Rev 20:10, 14), the deathless New Heaven and New Earth will be fully come and Paradise, finally, restored:

> Look! God's dwelling place is now among the people, and he will dwell with them. They will be his people, and God himself will be with them and be their God. "He will wipe every tear from their eyes. There will be no more death or mourning or crying or pain, for the old order of things has passed away." He who was seated on the throne said, "I am making everything new!" (Rev 21:3–5)

2.

As should be obvious in my telling of the gospel story, I've tried to emphasize the conflict between Christ and Satan, particularly in the way Satan comes to control the power of death and how Christ eventually comes to take this power away. In telling the story in this manner I'm attempting to illuminate a thread in the gospel narrative that suggests that salvation might involve something more than the forgiveness of sins. That is, there is nothing in the biblically driven account above that speaks to the necessity of a blood sacrifice to make atonement in order to appease a holy and wrathful God. In the telling above, salvation is about *rescue* and *emancipation*, Jesus setting humanity free from the dark powers of death and the devil. And though this emphasis might seem strange to many Protestants, this story is very biblical, as I tried to highlight. In short, while atonement and the forgiveness of sins are a part of the gospel story, the Bible also comments extensively about the role of death as the "power of the devil" in our lives, which are facets of salvation that we tend to overlook.

3.

The gospel account above—in which the conflict between Christ and the devil takes pride of place—is a telling that emphasizes what are known as Christus Victor themes. And while these themes are not routinely empha- sized in many modern Protestant traditions, these were the themes accented for the first thousand years of the church as Christians shared the gospel story. During that time period, Christians considered salvation to be about liberation from dark spiritual forces—liberation from sin, yes, but also from death and the devil. The seminal work of Gustaf Aulén has done much to recover this understanding of the early church:

> [Christus Victor's] central theme is the idea of the Atonement as a Divine conflict and victory; Christ—Christus Victor—fights against and triumphs over the evil powers of the world, the "ty- rants" under which mankind is in bondage and suffering, and in Him God reconciles the world to Himself.[1]

As we've seen, the main "tyrants" are described in the Bible as three practically interchangeable forces: sin, death, and the devil—the unholy Trinity. In Christus Victor theology salvation comes when Christ sets us free from these forces. Aulén elaborates on this understanding:

1. Aulén, *Christus Victor*, 4.

> The work of Christ is first and foremost a victory over the pow-
> ers which hold mankind in bondage: sin, death, and the devil.
> These may be said to be in a measure personified, but in any
> case they are objective powers; and the victory of Christ creates
> a new situation, bringing their rule to an end, and setting men
> free from their dominion.[2]

This focus on cosmic combat may sound strange to many (more on that shortly), but if we want to possess a full and rich understanding of the gospels we'll need to incorporate this biblical material into our vision of what Jesus was doing in his life and ministry. In his book *Simply Jesus,* N. T. Wright gives a rich biblical account of how Jesus understood his mission and shares an insightful observation:

> Wherever we look, it appears that Jesus was aware of a great
> battle in which he was already involved and that would, before
> too long, reach some kind of climax.
>   This was not, it seems, the battle that his contemporaries, in-
> cluding his own followers, expected him to fight. It wasn't even
> the same *sort* of battle—though Jesus used the language of battle
> to describe it. Indeed, as the Sermon on the Mount seems to in-
> dicate, fighting itself, in the normal physical sense, was precisely
> what he was not going to do. There was a different kind of battle
> in the offing, a battle that had already begun. In this battle, it
> was by no means as clear as those around Jesus would have liked
> as to who was on which side, or indeed whether "sides" was the
> right way to look at things. The battle in question was a different
> sort of thing, because it had a different sort of enemy. . . . The
> battle Jesus was fighting was against the satan.[3]

4.

Given that we've made out death to be the primary predicament of the hu-man condition, the vision of salvation we will be working with in this book takes its cue from Christus Victor theology. That is to say, our discussions about salvation in the remainder of this book will have less to do with the forgiveness of sin than the view of salvation as liberation from dark powers. Our specific focus will be the emancipation discussed in Hebrews 2:14–15: being set free from our slavery to the fear of death. As noted in chapter 1,

2. Ibid., 20.
3. Wright, *Simply Jesus,* 119–20.

if the satanic forces in our lives spring forth from the fear of death, then emancipation from this fear will move us from darkness to light, into a life characterized by a perfect love that has cast out fear.

That said, all this talk about the devil may be worrisome. For many of us, discussions of the devil conjure up scenes from *The Exorcist*, *Paranormal Activity*, or some other demon-haunted film from Hollywood.

And the worries here aren't solely about religious hysteria, charismatic excess, or spiritual abuse. Some of the concerns are theological in nature. Specifically, why would an omnipotent God need to do battle with Satan to liberate a captive humanity? There is something about this vision of a cosmic conflict between Christ and the devil that suggests that Satan is God's equal. This smacks too much of a pagan dualism, with the counterbalanced forces of good and evil eternally struggling for supremacy. Why would God have to condescend to have dealings with the devil to bring about our salvation?

Beyond these theological worries, modern people in a scientific age also find it hard to swallow all this talk about a character they imagine to be decked out in a red suit, complete with horns and a pitchfork.

For all of these reasons—religious hysteria, worries over dualism, the rise of science—Christus Victor theology has been eclipsed in Western Christianity, particularly within the liberal strains of Christianity where there has been great effort to accommodate modern science. Aulén comments on this perspective:

> [Modern, "liberal" theologians were] inclined to be critical of the forms in which the patristic teaching had usually expressed itself. They disliked intensely the "mythological" language of the early church about Christ's redemptive work, and the realistic, often undeniably grotesque imagery, in which the victory of Christ over the devil, or the deception of the devil, was depicted in lurid colours. Thus the whole dramatic view [of Christus Victor] was branded as "mythological." The matter was settled. The patristic teaching was of inferior value, and could be summarily relegated to the nursery or the lumber-room of theology.[4]

Not much has changed. Consequently, if we are going to be working with a Christus Victor frame in this book, we'll need to address objections or worries along these lines.

How should we think about the devil?

---

4. Aulén, *Christus Victor*, 9–10.

5.

I want to offer two responses.

First, our focus in this book is narrow and concentrates on how death anxiety causes us to behave in selfish and violent ways. In chapter 1, we discussed in detail the psychological dynamics we are trying to analyze and how this psychology sits comfortably within the scientific worldview. In short, given that our primary point of interest is the role of death in human psychology, we need not pay much attention to "the devil." That is, our Christus Victor frame will focus mostly on the moral power of death in our lives and less on the power of the devil.

So for most of this book I will use "the devil" more as an adjective than a noun. When I refer to "the devil's works," I will be speaking about sin and evil, describing certain behaviors as "devilish" or "satanic." In other words, I will use references to the devil as language of moral disapproval.

But if that's all I'm doing, then why make use of this language? This leads me to my second response.

While I predominantly use the language of the devil/Satan as shorthand for moral disapproval, I do think these terms are useful in describing distributed and suprahuman moral forces and influences. Satan might not be a personalized agent, but I do believe there are moral forces that transcend individuals, forces that have a real causal effect on moral decision-making. Moreover, I think these forces can be internalized. In fact, I think they often *are* internalized, in ways that make the language of demonic "possession" useful. Again, N. T. Wright is helpful on this score, describing how modern, scientific skeptics typically respond to mentions of the devil:

> Many modern writers, understandably, have tried to marginalize this theme [of Christ's conflict and victory over the satan], but we can't expect to push aside such a central part of the tradition and make serious progress. It is, of course, difficult for most people in the modern Western world to know what to make of it all; that's one of the points on which the strong wind of modern skepticism has done its work well, and the shrill retort from "traditionalists," insisting on seeing everything in terms of "supernatural" issues, hardly helps either. As C. S. Lewis points out in the introduction to his famous *Screwtape Letters*, the modern world divides into those who are obsessed with demonic powers and those who mock them as outdated rubbish. Neither approach, Lewis insists, does justice to reality.

I'm with Lewis on this. Despite the caricatures, the obsession, and the sheer muddle that people often get themselves into on this subject, there is such a thing as a dark force that seems to take over people, movements, and sometimes whole countries, a force or (as it sometimes seems) a set of forces that can make people do things they would never normally do.[5]

Wright goes on to note how these forces are still recognizably at work in the world today, still exerting an influence on human moral affairs, despite our quibbles about the language:

You might have thought the history of the twentieth century would provide plenty of examples of this [i.e., a dark force taking over people, movements and countries], but many still choose to resist the conclusion—despite the increasing use in public life of the language of "force" (economic "forces," political "forces," peer "pressure," and so on).[6]

Still, is calling these forces "demonic" or "satanic" a bit too florid and unnecessary? Wright thinks not, and argues that the language of the demonic can do important moral work for us:

Without the perspective that sees evil as a dark force that stands behind human reality, the issue of "good" and "bad" in our world is easy to decipher. It is fatally easy, and I mean fatally easy, to typecast "people like us" as basically good and "people like them" as basically evil. This is a danger we in our day should be aware of, after the disastrous attempts by some Western leaders to speak about an "axis of evil" and then go to war to obliterate it. We turn ourselves into angels and "the other lot" into demons; we "demonize" our opponents. This is a convenient tool for avoiding to have to think, but it is disastrous for both our thinking and our behavior.

But when you take seriously the existence and malevolence of non-human forces that are capable of using "us" as well as "them" in the service of evil, the focus shifts. As the hazy and shadowy realities come into view, what we thought was clear and straightforward becomes blurred. Life becomes more complex, but arguably more realistic. The traditional lines of friend and foe are not so easy to draw. You can no longer assume that "that lot" are simply agents of the devil and "this lot"—us and our friends—are automatically on God's side. If there is an

5. Wright, *Simply Jesus*, 121–22.

6. Ibid., 122.

enemy at work, it is a subtle, cunning enemy, much too clever to allow itself to be identified simply with one person, one group, or one nation. Only twice in the gospel story does Jesus address "the satan" directly by that title: once when rebuking him in the temptation narrative (Matt. 4:10), and again when he is rebuking his closest associate (Mark 8:33) for resisting God's strange plan. The line between good and evil is clear at the level of God, on the one hand, and the satan on the other. It is much, much less clear as it passes through human beings, individually and collectively.[7]

From Wright's analysis we can see at least two benefits of retaining language that points to spiritual forces at work in human affairs. First, such language points to suprahuman forces—what the Bible refers to as "the principalities and powers"—that are difficult to reduce to isolated moral agents. And yet, because these spiritual forces have real causal effects upon human affairs, we need to reckon with them in some way. But why must we use the word *spiritual* to describe the forces? We'll address that issue more thoroughly in chapter 4, but for now suffice it to say that these forces are difficult to locate in any material way, and they tend to exert their moral influence within the realm of human subjective experience—our hearts, minds, and spirits.

A second reason to use this language, as Wright points out, is that it helps us shift the moral conversation to a plane where we are less prone to victimize and demonize each other. This is not to say we are hapless agents in the face of these forces. But it is helpful to recognize the malevolent winds that have the potential to carry individuals and whole populations along in their wake. In acknowledging these powerful forces, we can increase our empathy for others and help focus our efforts on changing the political, economic, and cultural institutions that embody systemic evil. Surely many of us have reflected on Nazi Germany and wondered if we would have been able, as individuals, to resist the dark spiritual and moral forces at work in that time and place. The biblical language regarding "the principalities and powers" helps us see morality as a Gestalt that is distributed throughout the entire web of human existence. In short, such perspectives clarify that in our moral struggles we should focus less on our conflicts with "flesh and blood" and more on our battle with the suprahuman forces that exert influence on human moral affairs. This allows us to take our cue from Paul:

> For we wrestle not against flesh and blood, but against prin-
> cipalities, against powers, against the rulers of the darkness

7. Ibid., 122–23.

of this world, against spiritual wickedness in high places. (Eph 6:12 KJV)

For our purposes in this book, the language of the "principalities and powers" will be used to describe how our slavery to the fear of death comes to manifest itself neurotically and in more repressed guises. We'll come to see, particularly in chapter 4, how in our quest for meaning and significance in the face of death we idolatrously come to serve, and are thus enslaved by, the principalities and powers—those institutions, vocations, ideologies, or lifeways that hold out the promise of durability and immortality. These attachments to the principalities and powers, driven as they are by death anxiety, become another manifestation of our slavery to the fear of death.

6.

In sum, the language regarding spiritual forces and powers will prove to be useful for a number of different reasons.

That said, for the most part in this book I will bracket questions regarding the reality of a literal personalized Satan. Again, my primary focus is death and how death creates moral failure. And though I might bracket here the question about a literal devil, I feel very comfortable describing how death creates *satanic* effects, violence in particular. In this I see my task as being descriptive in nature—an analysis of what is plainly observed by all, skeptic and believer alike. While we can debate the metaphysical backdrop, my focus will be upon the visible and empirical effects of death upon our moral lives and how those effects correlate with the biblical imagination. And as we'll see, this "correlation" isn't abstract but very empirical. Regardless, I encourage all readers, from across the theological spectrum, to take my descriptions in this book and integrate them with their own views regarding the existence of Satan and the nature of our spiritual conflict. Working as I am from a psychological vantage point, nothing that I'll describe precludes or necessitates Satan's existence. There will be plenty of room for both liberal and conservative theological perspectives at the end of the book.

7.

Let's conclude Part 1 with a positive vision. If Christus Victor theology emphasizes our emancipation from the dark spiritual forces that hold us captive, what exactly does this victory look like? How is it experienced? More specifically, given our focus on the slavery to death, what does it mean to be set free from this bondage to the fear of death as described in Hebrews 2:14–15?

For the Orthodox, the key sign of our liberation from sin, death, and the devil is the experience of a love set free from self-interest and fear. As the Orthodox theologian John Romanides notes, there is a distinction "between those who live according to Satan and death and those who struggle in Christ to attain to unselfish love that is free of self-interest and necessity."[8] And what is this distinction? The presence of a fearless love: "The salvation of man is dependent upon how much, under the guidance of God, he is capable of exercising himself in the cultivation of a genuine, unselfish, and unconstrained love for God and his fellow man."[9] The struggle here—the distinction between life and death—is the battle between love and self-interest, a selfishness that is only natural given our mortal nature and the inevitability of death. Romanides writes,

> Love that is free of self-interest and necessity fears nothing. . . . Any perceived threat automatically triggers fear and uneasiness. Fear does not allow a man to be perfected in love. . . . Being under the sway of death and not having real and correct faith in God, man is anxious over everything and is ruled by selfish bodily and psychological motives and, thus, he is unable to love unselfishly and freely. He loves and has faith according to what he perceives to be to his own advantage. . . . Thus, he is deprived of his original destiny and is off the mark spiritually. In biblical language, these failures and deviations are called sins. The fountain of man's personal sin is the power of death that is in the hands of the devil and in man's own willing submission to him.[10]

Salvation, then, is being set free from this self-interest. The sign of our progress is the advent of love in our lives. A final word from Romanides:

> Just as God, above all, is free of every need and self-interest, the spiritual man who has the Spirit struggles and becomes perfected in the love according to Christ, love that is delivered of all need and self-interest.[11]

To be set free from the slavery to the fear of death is to be liberated from self-interest in the act of genuine love. Thus the sign of Christ's victory in our lives over sin, death, and the devil is the experience and expression of love. This is resurrection and life.

As 1 John 3:14 describes, love is the moment when we "move from death to life."

8. Romanides, *Ancestral Sin*, 133.

9. Ibid., 121.

10. Ibid., 116–17.

11. Ibid., 153.

PART 2

"Held in Slavery by Their Fear of Death"

Chapter 3

The Denial of Death

1.

My hope is that our brief discussion of the Orthodox tradition has helped readers to at least entertain the reversal I outlined in Part 1: that death is at the center of the human predicament and that the fear of death is the primary source of sin in our lives, the "power of the devil." Similarly, I hope readers are now able to also consider the emphasis of Christus Victor theology, the notion that salvation involves emancipation from dark forces that hold us captive. In light of our focus on death, salvation is effected when Christ breaks the hold of death on our lives. Psychologically speaking, in the words of Chrysostom, the one who does not fear death is found to be free, "outside the tyranny of the devil." Free of this tyranny, the fear of death can no longer be used to catalyze our natural instincts for self-preservation into selfish and violent practices. More, by casting out this fear we make possible the experience of love, the ability to postpone or sacrifice our self-interest for the sake of others and the world.

2.

Here in Part 2 we turn from theology to psychology. My goal in Part 2 is to show how psychological science confirms and informs the theological perspectives described in Part 1. We've already seen some hints of this when we noted how the Orthodox vision of ancestral sin converges on biological and sociological perspectives relating survival fears to selfishness and violence. But there is much, much more to be said, and thus our journey in Part 2 will go deeper.

3.

The psychological story I will share has two distinct parts, each corresponding to different forms of anxiety, different manifestations of fear, our fear of death in particular. Within the psychoanalytic tradition these two fears are characterized as *basic anxiety* and *neurotic anxiety*. We will contrast how these two types of anxiety manifest in our lives and also explore how death relates to each.

We've already described the essential shape of basic anxiety, but let's review. Basic anxiety is the anxiety of biological survival, the anxiety of our fight-or-flight response, the anxiety associated with vigilantly monitoring threats in our physical environment. Basic anxiety is connected to the survival instincts we have as biodegradable animals in a world of real or potential scarcity. The logic here, as we've noted, is fairly straightforward: in the face of survival threats, our self-interest intensifies. And if the situation becomes dire, violence breaks out.

But little of this seems to be indicative of a slavery to the fear of death, particularly in affluent parts of the world where nearly everyone has enough resources to meet their basic biological needs. How is death creating selfishness and violence in these situations of relative abundance?

This question turns us towards a different sort of anxiety—neurotic anxiety. Unlike basic anxiety, neurotic anxiety isn't involved in monitoring environmental threats and resources. Rather, it is characterized by worries, fears, and apprehensions associated with our self-concept, much of which is driven by how we compare ourselves to those in our social world. Feelings of insecurity, low self-esteem, obsessions, perfectionism, ambitiousness, envy, narcissism, jealousy, rivalry, competitiveness, self-consciousness, guilt, and shame are all examples of neurotic anxiety, and they all relate to how we evaluate ourselves in our own eyes and the eyes of others. Perhaps we worry about weighing too much or masturbating too much, or we feel insecure for not making as much money as our neighbors. On the flip side, feelings of superiority, contempt, and pride are also forms of neurotic anxiety. In short, neurotic anxiety sits at the root of our experience of self-esteem, the motive force behind our vigilant monitoring of how we compare to others and to cultural standards, for good or ill. Here in Part 2, I argue that our slavery to the fear of death often manifests *in the form of neurotic anxiety,* an anxiety that determines how we form our identities and pursue meaning in the world. So while Part 1 discussed how basic anxiety produces sinful outcomes in Hobbesian and Darwinian situations, Part 2 will focus on neurotic anxiety and how all of us—rich and poor alike—are enslaved by a fear of death, even if we live in affluent societies.

4.

To understand how death anxiety in the Western world has taken on a more neurotic character, it might be helpful to step back and discuss how technological and medical advances over the last two hundred years have radically altered how we relate to the reality of death. Specifically, prior to the industrial revolution and the advent of modern medicine, our experience of death was more direct and immediate. Death was a daily reality. Consequently, the anxiety associated with death was less neurotic and more basic in nature. When people live life close to the bone, they don't have a lot of energy to waste on worrying about keeping up with the Joneses or having a bad hair day. Surviving the day is trouble enough.

The situation today in more affluent parts of the world is very different. Technology, market economies, scientific agriculture, and advanced medicine have largely insulated us from death. We modern people rarely face death in our day-to-day lives. Consequently, we rarely give death any thought at all. In fact, if we do take time to contemplate death, others might think that we have a morbid or depressive temperament. So it's not just that we *don't* think of death, it's that we *shouldn't* think of death. And it's here, with this reticence, that we catch our first hint that our modern relationship with death has taken a neurotic turn.

This reticence to dwell upon death is symptomatic of what Geoffrey Gorer has called "the pornography of death,"[1] the sense that death has become an illicit subject, too unseemly for public discussion or reflection. Death, like pornography, should be hidden from view.

How did this avoidance come about? While there were many factors that led to its development, we can note three particularly influential shifts.

First, changes occurred in our relationship to our food. In agrarian and herding cultures there was a close association between death and food. People literally killed their own food—killed it, bled it, skinned it, prepared it, cooked it, and ate it, often with only a few minutes separating

1. Gorer, *Death, Grief, and Mourning,* 197–98.

each step. The association between death and food couldn't have been any closer. Moreover, the food was full of reminders that it was once a living thing—bones, for example. Compare that life and that bony food with the experience of eating, say, a Chicken McNugget.

In our age, death has become radically disassociated with our food consumption. We don't personally kill the animals we eat. Death occurs somewhere else—out of sight, out of awareness. Food just magically appears, disconnected from life and death. Further, when we do eat meat, as with the Chicken McNugget example, we have few signs that it was once a chicken, a living animal. In short, our relationship with our food has been radically emptied of all death-reminders.

Second, changes have also occurred in how and where we die. In the past, family members cared for the sick, doctors made house visits (though they couldn't do much to help), and the ill, injured, and elderly died at home. People witnessed mothers and babies dying tragically in childbirth. Death, in short, was a routine part of family life and regularly found and encountered in the home.

In addition, after death families prepared the body and buried their loved ones in family or church plots. Consequently, by the time people reached their own deaths, they had already personally cared for, handled, and buried many lifeless bodies. Every residence was both a hospital and funeral home. Just about every female child had served as a hospice nurse. Just about every male child had helped dig a grave.

All this changed with the rise of the modern hospital. With the advent of modern technological medicine, death was taken out of the home and moved into hospitals. In the face of this change the funeral industry began to create "funeral homes"; thus the burial process was also removed from households and the daily lives of families. "Specialists" started to handle sickness, hospice care, and death. And with funeral services no longer taking place in the parlor of the home, magazines of this era began to propose that the parlor be reclaimed from the dead and returned to the living. To signal this, to erase the memory of the dead, parlors became "living rooms." Yes, parlors still exist today, but mainly in *funeral* homes.

A third change, one also associated with the rise of the funeral industry, involved the relocation of cemeteries. In times past the dead were buried on family land or in cemeteries adjacent to churches that doubled as schools and public gathering spaces—an arrangement that still exists in some historic sites. In short, people lived next door to cemeteries. The home, the church, the school, and the public square were all a stone's throw away from the dead. Again, death was a constant companion.

But with the rise of the modern funeral industry, cemeteries were gradually distanced from homes, churches, schools, and public squares. They moved from the center of life to the periphery—physically, culturally, and psychologically. Death was effectively banished from our field of view.

All of these cultural changes minimized our encounter with death in daily life. But these cultural shifts pale in comparison to how our affluence and the power of modern medicine have been steadily increasing life expectancy. Over a hundred yeas ago the leading causes of death were communicable diseases and infections, but today, in the industrialized world, the leading causes of death are degenerative diseases of old age like heart disease and cancer. This shift has profoundly altered our experience of death. Basically, we've come to *expect* to live to a ripe old age. Given this expectation, when death comes sooner we experience a radical disruption, as if something has gone *wrong*. Despite the fact that we know we are biological creatures and that death is inevitable, death comes as a shock to us, whereas it rarely, if ever, shocked our forebears. And this shock is a symptom of our neurotic relationship with death.

5.

All these advances that delay our eventual death appear to be a good thing, and they are, but death really hasn't gone anywhere. What has happened is that all these advances have created an illusion of *immortality*, making it feel as though death has been banished from our lives. Because as a day-to-day reality, it largely has been. This is why speaking of death is generally avoided, why death is pornographic. Pausing to note death's existence destroys the illusion. Rather than face the reality of death—which takes some effort in our society, given how death has been delayed—it's easier to indulge the collective illusion of a deathless society.

Such pretending wouldn't be so bad if it were not for the fact that this psychological and social avoidance is driven by an underlying neurotic anxiety. And where there is fear and anxiety, there is opportunity to be manipulated and tempted. In an attempt to manage or reduce our anxiety, we are driven to embrace distractions, entertainments, and comforts. The illusion of a deathless society can only be maintained by a vast industry of such distractions and entertainments.

One of the more incisive descriptions of the American culture of death avoidance is given by the theologian Arthur McGill in his book *Death and Life: An American Theology*, which he begins by observing that "Americans like to appear as if they give death hardly any thought at all."[2] The American lifestyle is thus "for people to create a living world where death seems abnormal and accidental. [Americans] must create a living world where life is so full, so secure, and so rich with possibilities that it gives no hint of death and deprivation."[3]

We accomplish this feat, according to McGill, through acts of death avoidance. Americans live with "the conviction that the lives we live are not essentially and intrinsically mortal."[4] But this is a neurotic fantasy. McGill calls it a "dream," an "illusory realm of success."[5]

So how is this illusion maintained? According to McGill, "Americans accomplish this illusion by devoting themselves to expunging from their lives every appearance, every intimation of death. . . . All traces of weakness, debility, ugliness and helplessness must be kept away from every part of a person's life. The task must be done every single day if such persons really are to convince us that they do not carry the smell of death within them."[6]

McGill's comments depict how the American success ethos—the cultural expectation to be "fine"—is driven by an underlying existential fear. Here we see slavery to the fear of death, but it's less direct and more neurotic in nature, now more unconscious than conscious. This unconscious avoidance supports the collective pretending, the psychic game that allows us to avoid a direct confrontation with our own mortality. McGill explains that through these acts of avoidance "Americans are able to shield themselves from the awfulness of life, from the torment and devastation which always threaten to overwhelm their sensitivity."[7]

It's also important to note that American religion plays a part in supporting the cultural illusion. Vast portions of American Christianity are aimed at propping up the illusion, giving religious sanction to American death avoidance. We see this in the triumphalism within many sectors of Christianity—the almost manic optimism of church culture that cannot

2. McGill, *Death and Life*, 13.

3. Ibid., 18.

4. Ibid., 27.

5. Ibid., 35.

6. Ibid., 26.

7. Ibid., 41.

admit any hint of debility, disease, death, or decay. These churches are filled with smiling cheerful people who respond with "Fine!" to any inquiry regarding their social, financial, emotional, physical, or spiritual well-being. Due to many churches' explicit and implicit religious sanctioning of the American success ethos, church members become too afraid to show each other their weakness, brokenness, failure, and vulnerability. Such admissions are avoided, as they threaten to expose the neurotic lie that sits at the heart of Christian culture and American society—that death doesn't exist. Consider this analysis from Walter Brueggemann regarding why many Christian churches avoid the use of the lament psalms in worship:

> It is a curious fact that the church has, by and large, continued to sing songs of orientation in a world increasingly experienced as disoriented. . . .
>
> . . . It is my judgment that this action of the church is less an evangelical defiance guided by faith, and much more a frightened, numb denial and deception that does not want to acknowledge or experience the disorientation of life. The reason for such relentless affirmation of orientation seems to me, not from faith, but from the wishful optimism of our culture. Such a denial and cover-up, which I take it to be, is an odd inclination for passionate Bible users, given the larger number of psalms that are songs of lament, protest, and complaint about an incoherence that is experienced in the world. . . .
>
> I think that serious religious use of the lament psalms has been minimal because we have believed that faith does not mean to acknowledge and embrace negativity. We have thought that acknowledgment of negativity was somehow an act of unfaith, as though the very speech about it conceded too much about God's "loss of control."
>
> The point to be urged here is this: The use of these "psalms of darkness" may be judged by the world to be *acts of unfaith and failure,* but for the trusting community, their use is *an act of bold faith.* . . .[8]

It's interesting that Brueggemann, a biblical scholar, uses the language of neuroses and repression. The avoidance of the lament psalms is a "frightened, numb denial and deception," a "cover-up" that "does not mean to acknowledge and embrace negativity." If this is so (and what Brueggemann describes has certainly been my experience in American churches), then we find American Christianity firmly under "the power of the devil," enslaved to the fear of death.

8. Brueggemann, *Message of the Psalms,* 51–52.

What are the social and psychological contours of this slavery? The culture of death avoidance creates a suite of demands, most importantly the demand to conceal any weakness, failure, and disability. In the words of McGill,

> The most crucial task is for people to create a living world where death seems abnormal and accidental. They must create a living world where life is so full, so secure, and so rich with possibilities that it gives no hint of death and deprivation. . . . According to this duty, a person must try to live in such a way that he or she does not carry the marks of death, does not exhibit any hint of the failure of life. A person must try to prove by his or her own existence that failure does not belong essentially to life. Failure is an accident, a remediable breakdown of the system.[9]

McGill's argument is that what we tend to call "success" in American culture is often a neurotic delusion, a defense mechanism we use to deny the reality of death, both in our lives and the lives of others. The cultural expectation to be "fine" is at root an ethic of death avoidance:

> Every American is thus ingrained with the duty to look well, to seem fine, to exclude from the fabric of his or her normal life any evidence of decay and death and helplessness. The ethic I have outlined here is often called the ethic of success. I prefer to call it the ethic of avoidance. . . . Persons are considered a success not because they attain some remarkable goal, but because their lives do not betray marks of failure or depression, helplessness or sickness. When they are asked how they are, they really can say and really do say, "Fine . . . fine."[10]

What this duty creates is a shallow, superficial, and inauthentic culture, a culture driven to maintain social appearances and devoid of deep and authentic relationality. By refusing to share our weaknesses and failures with others—by insisting we are "fine"—we all become rugged individualists, struggling alone to make the best of it. We never express our needs to others; we never invite others into our lives. We are happy to help others but are loathe in this culture of death avoidance *to ask for help*. And when everyone plays this game, no one helps. As a result, the illusion of collective "fineness"—the illusion of a deathless society—is confirmed and maintained.

Beyond maintaining personal appearances, the culture of death avoidance demands that reminders of death, disability, age, failure, and weakness

---

9. McGill, *Death and Life*, 18.

10. Ibid., 19–20.

be removed from public view. The poor, old, disabled, sick, and needy are pushed to the edges of public life and polity, since exposure to these people feels disruptive and unseemly. We like our streets looking spotless and deathless, cleansed of anyone who destroys the carefully cultivated and manicured illusion. These sorts of people are pornographic, reminders of something illicit that shouldn't appear in public view. A final word from McGill:

> Why is there this passion to gather people into the arena of true life and to remove from them all marks of sickness and debility? Because many Americans have to create a society which does not cause or require debility and death. Life, life, and more life— that is the only horizon within which these Americans want to live. Epidemics of sickness, economic disasters bringing mass starvation, social violence and disorder threatening at every street corner—if any such things were to happen, then death would no longer be outside of life, be accidental to life. Then, the American venture of nice homes, clean streets, decent manners, and daily security would prove to be false.[11]

In summary, we find in McGill's analysis of American culture a description of what a slavery to the fear of death looks like when this fear takes a neurotic form. In contemporary American culture our slavery to the fear of death produces superficial consumerism, a fetish for managing appearances, inauthentic relationships, triumphalistic religion, and the eclipse of personal and societal empathy. These are the "works of the devil" in our lives, works produced by our slavery to the fear of death.

And as if this isn't enough, it gets worse. Our slavery to the fear of death goes even deeper.

6.

I want to turn now to one of the seminal works in the field of psychology, Ernest Becker's book *The Denial of Death* and its sequel, *Escape from Evil.* Perhaps no psychological work has so thoroughly analyzed how our neurotic fears of death shape our individual identities and society at large. In addition, thanks to empirically minded psychologists working with what is called terror management theory (a theory inspired by Becker's work), Becker's insights have received significant empirical confirmation in the laboratory.

11. Ibid., 21.

Becker begins his analysis in *The Denial of Death* by focusing on our need for self-esteem, our desire for our life to be significant and meaningful—both to ourselves and to others. He describes this as a striving for *heroism*, suggesting that "our central calling, our main task on this planet, is the heroic."[12]

This heroism—a feeling of significance—is achieved by following cultural pathways that mark a life, within any given culture, as both admirable and well lived. More, this heroism is found in a life that "makes a difference" by creating or being a part of something that "lasts":

> . . . this is what a society is and always has been: a symbolic action system, a structure of statuses and roles, customs and rules for behavior, designed to serve as a vehicle for earthly heroism. Each script is somewhat unique, each culture has a different hero system. . . . But each cultural system is a dramatization of earthly heroics; each system cuts out roles for performances of various degrees of heroism. . . .
>
> It doesn't matter whether the cultural hero-system is frankly magical, religious, and primitive or secular, scientific, and civilized. It is still a mythical hero-system in which people serve in order to earn a feeling of primary value, of cosmic specialness, of ultimate usefulness to creation, of unshakable meaning. They earn this feeling by carving out a place in nature, by building an edifice that reflects human value: a temple, a cathedral, a totem pole, a skyscraper, a family that spans three generations. The hope and belief is that the things that man creates in society are of lasting worth and meaning, that they outlive or outshine death and decay, that man and his products count.[13]

Let me give a concrete and personal example of this. I'm an American college professor and this lays out a "hero system" that can give my life significance and meaning. That is, there are various things I can do as a professor to be "successful" and to feel good about myself. For example, I can publish articles and acquire positive student evaluations of my classroom performance. Such things suggest that I am "good" at what I do. As a result, I get a sense of self-esteem, a sense that my life "matters." We all live within a particular hero system, and each system participates in various ways (even as a hero system of dissent[14]) within the overarching cultural hero system.

12. Becker, *Denial of Death*, 1.

13. Ibid., 4–5.

14. Even rebels and radicals are using the hero system of the dominant culture as a reference point in a sort of figure/ground reversal.

So far, so good. We all strive to be "heroic," to achieve self-esteem in lesser or greater ways by comparing ourselves to some value system rooted in our culture. But what is motivating this need for heroism?

Becker argues that the quest for self-esteem is fundamentally an attempt to cope with the terror of death: "heroism is first and foremost a reflex of the terror of death."[15] He implies that culture itself, which determines the routes toward heroism, is massively engaged in the repression of death awareness. As Becker notes, "cultures are fundamentally and basically styles of heroic death denial."[16]

That's a pretty big claim. How does Becker support that notion?

From his point of view, the higher cognitive and symbolic capacities of humans make our workaday lives existentially unbearable. The specter of death looms over all, making a mockery of our life projects. Our primal instincts for self-preservation come up short in the face of our cognitive capacities, which continually remind us that death is unavoidable. This clash between our self-preservation instinct and our ever-present death awareness creates an extreme burden of anxiety that other animals are spared:

> The knowledge of death is reflective and conceptual, and animals are spared it. They live and they disappear with the same thoughtlessness: a few minutes of fear, a few seconds of anguish, and it is over. But to live a whole lifetime with the fate of death haunting one's dreams and even the most sun-filled days—that's something else. It is only if you let the full weight of this paradox sink down on your mind and feelings that you can realize what an impossible situation it is for an animal to be in.[17]

This experiential burden threatens madness or despair. How do we make life "count" in the face of death? Here is where cultural hero systems step in to provide paths toward death transcendence—a means toward a symbolic (or literal) immortality. Life achieves significance and meaning when we participate in these "greater goods" that can transcend our finite existence. For example, my life is deemed meaningful because my children outlive me, or I wrote a book, or I helped the company have its best quarter of the year. Child, book, and company are all forms of "immortality," ways to continue living into the future in an effort to "defeat" death.

The upshot of this analysis—that we strive for a heroic existence and that cultural hero systems help us cope with the terror of death—is that our identities are being driven, deep down, by death anxiety.

15. Becker, *Denial of Death*, 11.
16. Becker, *Escape from Evil*, 125.
17. Becker, *Denial of Death*, 27.

And here is where we see just how far down the rabbit hole we have gone in following the thread of death anxiety, where we come face to face with our enslavement to the fear of death. Ponder again the verdict of Hebrews 2:14–15: What does it mean to say that we are enslaved—all our lives—to the fear of death? Becker helps us see this slavery, suggesting that our sense of life meaning and self-esteem, the very bedrock of our identities, are actually forms of *death denial*, an existential defense mechanism, an illusion to help us avoid the full force of our existential predicament.

This is why Becker calls human character—our personal route toward self-esteem—a *lie*. Our identity is a *lie* because it is a fundamental dishonesty, in the moment, about our true existential situation. This lie obscures the fact that our self-esteem is borrowed, that it rests upon a cultural hero system. More, the lie hides the fact that our self-esteem is fundamentally a form of idolatry, a service rendered to the cultural hero system—what the Bible calls a principality and power.

But this dishonesty is *vital* in that it is necessary in order for the human animal to continue on in the face of death. Again, the existential burden that death places upon us is impossible to carry. Consequently, culture steps in to lighten our load, largely through repression and sublimation. As we've discussed, cultural heroics provide us with routes of identity formation. Here Becker comments on these dynamics:

> We called one's life style a vital lie, and now we can understand better why we said it was vital: it is a *necessary* and basic dishonesty about oneself and one's whole situation. . . . We don't want to admit that we are fundamentally dishonest about reality, that we do not really control our own lives. We don't want to admit that we do not stand alone, that we always rely on something that transcends us, some system of ideas and powers in which we are embedded and which support us. This power is not obvious. It need not be overtly a god or openly a stronger person, but it can be the power of an all-absorbing activity, a passion, a dedication to a game, a way of life, that like a comfortable web keeps a person buoyed up and ignorant of himself, of the fact that he does not rest on his own center. All of us are driven to be supported in a self-forgetful way, ignorant of what energies we really draw on, of the kind of lie we have fashioned in order to live securely and serenely. Augustine was a master analyst of this, as were Kierkegaard, Scheler, and Tillich in our day. They saw that man could strut and boast all he wanted, but that he really drew his "courage to be" from a god, a string of sexual

conquests, a Big Brother, a flag, the proletariat, and the fetish of money and the size of a bank balance.

The defenses that form a person's character support a grand illusion, and when we grasp this we can understand the full drivenness of man. He is driven away from himself, from self-knowledge, self-reflection. He is driven toward things that support the lie of his character, his automatic equanimity.[18]

And so we arrive at a startling, radical, and destabilizing conclusion: we are enslaved to the fear of death because the basis of our identities—all the ways we define ourselves and make meaning with our lives—is revealed to be an illusion, a lie, an obfuscation, a neurotic defense mechanism involved in death repression. Death saturates every aspect of our personhood.

This means that our slavery to the fear of death is insidious and hard to eradicate. It's difficult to simply "opt out," because the problem is too pervasive and goes too deep. Radical measures are necessary. This predicament gives us a glimpse into why the biblical authors speak of conversion and discipleship as a *death*—our identities are too saturated with death to be rehabilitated as they stand. Consequently, in order to fully and completely confront our slavery to the fear of death, we must "die" to our entire identity as it is currently configured. Moreover, we must "die" to the overarching cultural hero system, the way everyone around us makes meaning and defines success and significance. And that is a terrifying prospect. This is a renunciation on a grand scale where the "old man" (a death-saturated identity producing sinful attitudes and behaviors) is "buried" so that a "new creation" (an identity rooted in Christ) can be raised to take its place.

7.

All this might sound rather dramatic and overblown. Are such drastic measures really necessary? Do we really need to overhaul our entire identity to experience authentic community and love? What's the problem with trying to secure cultural goods and pursue cultural values, even if these quests are motivated by a latent death anxiety? Isn't there some intrinsic goodness in all these things?

Becker would affirm that death anxiety isn't all bad. Again, the general (though not exclusively so) defense mechanism at work here is sublimation, the channeling of our anxieties into productive and valued outlets. Maybe a person did spend an entire lifetime building up a company in the quest for meaning and significance. But the fruits of that labor likely made the world

18. Ibid., 55–56.

a better place. Maybe another was an artist who poured time and effort into creative outlets. And those works of art, music, and literature probably enhanced the world's beauty. And maybe a third sought self-esteem from writing a book and seeing it in print. And people read that book and were blessed by its content. In short, even if anxiety pervades our motives, the products of this anxiety can be pretty great.

So the cultural hero system and the life lived in pursuing cultural heroics are not wholly bankrupt. In fact, it's the great genius of the cultural hero system that it channels our deepest fears into such positive directions. That's sort of the point. Becker follows Freud in suggesting that it's our neurotic anxiety that makes us human and provides the fuel for all our creative cultural output.[19] Like self-interest in capitalism, the hero system enables something unsavory—a desire for significance in the face of death—to be harnessed and channeled into something useful and creative.

But there is a darkness at the heart of this dynamic, and it's this darkness that concerns us here. To be sure, nothing is wrong with going to work, creating art, or writing books—these are great goods, particularly when life is going well. But during times of stress or threat, the darkness tends to manifest. For example, I'm writing this book in the midst of the greatest economic downturn since the Great Depression. Is it surprising, in light of these hard times, that American political discourse has degenerated into rage, paranoia, suspicion, and hysteria? As we discussed in Part 1, during times of want and scarcity our worries over self-preservation tend to set us against each other. When we feel there are not enough resources to go around, preserving our piece of the pie, our slice of the American Dream, becomes vitally important. During these times of real, potential, or perceived scarcity we become increasingly indifferent to the competing claims of others and unwilling to make personal sacrifices to reach toward a common and greater good.

This example illustrates how basic anxiety leads to aggression. But does neurotic anxiety, the anxiety that drives our quest for self-esteem in the face of death, also prompt violence?

Yes, it does. A large part of Ernest Becker's reputation among psychologists stems from his articulation of this connection, a connection that has been supported by empirical research.[20] This link between neurotic

19. The difference is that whereas Freud rooted this anxiety in a libidinal conflict, Becker rooted it in our existential predicament. But for both the neurotic anxiety was largely unconscious and sublimated.

20. Much of Becker's seminal insights—the role of self-esteem in repressing death anxiety and how the defense of cultural hero systems leads to violence—has been supported by the empirical work investigating what is called terror management theory.

anxiety and violence is important because without it we might assume that basic anxiety is our only moral worry and that violence occurs only in times of scarcity. But if neurotic anxiety also produces violence, then there is no escape. Neurotic anxiety builds our sense of identity as we pursue self-esteem and meaning in the face of death, which means that if neurotic anxiety is linked to violence, then violence is an *intrinsic* feature of our identity. In other words, violence is not triggered only by external causes, during times of lack and scarcity. Violence also bubbles up from *within*.

How so? How exactly does neurotic anxiety produce violence?

Becker explores the identity-violence connection and also outlines the great tragedy of human existence in *Escape from Evil*, his sequel to *The Denial of Death*. As we discussed above, Becker believes that our lives are experienced as significant because we create cultural hero systems. And yet, every culture has its own values and goods—its own hero system that defines what a "meaningful" life looks like. This poses a problem: a hero system only "works" if we experience it as immune to death, as something eternal and timeless. At the very least, the system must be more durable than a human body.

Basically, for a hero system to "work," for it to give us a sense of security and permanence in the face of death, we need to experience it as absolute, unassailable, true, eternal, transcendent, and ultimate. This belief is threatened when we come into contact with cultural outsiders who espouse different values. The existence of other ways of life, other values, and other paths by which to pursue significance threaten to relativize our culture's unique values. That is, we find in our encounter with cultural outsiders that our "way of life" is just one among many in the marketplace of worldviews. This discovery shakes our confidence that our particular worldview is both true and eternal. If there are many hero systems, how can we be sure that our culture's specific system is durable and eternal in the face of death? If our cultural lifeways are revealed to be arbitrary and relative, then their function as existential lifeboats—as cultural containers of immortality that we can pour our lives into—is radically compromised.

In short, alternative hero systems—other values, worldviews, and ways of life—threaten to undo everything that has made our lives feel significant, meaningful, and secure in the face of death. The ideological Other—usually some out-group member who has different values and beliefs from our own—presents us with an implicit critique of our personal hero system. This threatens us to the core, attacks the very source of our self-esteem. This

See Solomon, Greenberg, and Pyszczynski, "Cultural Animal," for a review of the relevant theory and empirical findings.

means that the ideological Other—the out-group member who is simply different from us—doesn't really have to do anything particularly threatening. His or her mere *existence* is enough to menace us. Outgroup members represent, on the edges of our awareness, a dissenting voice that suggests that the way we've constructed our identities and the criteria we've used to manage our self-esteem are not eternal and transcendent but are instead arbitrary human fictions.

So what do we do in the face of that threat? Simply stated, we demonize these people. Rather than endure existential discomfort, it's easier to double down on our worldview and to see those different from us as malevolent agents.[21] We aggress against these "others." In mild forms, we view them as confused or mistaken. More severely, they grow to become enemies we have to forcibly eliminate. Becker describes this dynamic:

> The thing that feeds the great destructiveness of history is that men give their entire allegiance to their own group; and each group is a codified hero system. Which is another way of saying that societies are standardized systems of death denial; they give structure to the formulas for heroic transcendence. . . .[22]

> Cultures are fundamentally and basically *styles of heroic death denial*. We can then ask empirically, it seems to me, what are the costs of such denials of death, because we know how these denials are structured into styles of life. These costs can be tallied roughly in two ways: in terms of the tyranny practiced within the society, and in terms of the victimage practiced against aliens or "enemies" outside it. . . .[23]

In the next chapter we'll discuss in a bit more detail how the principalities and powers fit into this picture. For now let us simply register Becker's final point: in order to protect the worldview that gives our life grounding and significance, we are driven to victimize out-group members and persecute those who are different.

What all of this means is that neurotic anxiety produces violence as much as basic anxiety. In fact, neurotic anxiety might be much, much worse. In his study on the origins and psychological roots of human evil, the psychologist Roy Baumeister has observed that most of the violence in the modern era can be attributed to the idealism found in national mythologies

---

21. Those working with terror management theory call this aggression "worldview defense." See Solomon, Greenberg, and Pyszczynski, "Cultural Animal."

22. Becker, *Escape from Evil*, 153–54.

23. Ibid., 125.

and ideological movements.[24] Worldviews, because of the ways in which they ground our being in the face of death, lead us to kill. And even at their mildest, worldviews cause us to marginalize and exclude out-group members—the beginnings of the slow process of dehumanization and demonization.

8.

To conclude this chapter, what I find stunning and remarkable about Becker's work is how psychology has once again converged upon the biblical imagination. In exploring the psychological associations between neurotic forms of death anxiety and violence, we once again uncover intimate links between sin, death, and the devil. What we find in Becker is how the fear of death, in both its basic and neurotic forms, is implicated across the spectrum of moral failure—from small acts of selfishness to genocide.

We find, once again, that our slavery to the fear of death produces sin and "the works of the devil."

---

24. Baumeister, *Evil: Inside Human Violence and Cruelty.*

Chapter 4

The Principalities and Powers

1.

In Part 1 we discussed the theology of Christus Victor, which views salvation as the outcome of Christ winning a victory over the dark forces that hold us captive—Satan and death, in particular. In chapter 3 we focused specifically on our captivity to death, how a slavery to the fear of death saturates our culture and our identities. In this chapter, though our focus will remain on death, I'd like to unpack how we might understand, psychologically speaking, what it means to be held captive by Satan.

The key idea here is that our slavery to the fear of death often manifests as *idolatry*, as service rendered to suprahuman forces. To reiterate what we discussed in the previous chapter, in order to feel significant in the face of death we engage in cultural heroics. More often than not we achieve these heroics, this sense of meaning and significance, by serving various institutions or ideologies in our world—what the Bible calls the "principalities and powers." When serving these principalities and powers we can become "possessed" by them, internalizing the spirituality of their culture and ruling ethos. Viewed through the Christus Victor frame, being set free from the slavery to the fear of death involves a confrontation with these forms of "possession" and idolatry. We must be set free from their spirituality; we must undergo an "exorcism" as it were. We must give up these

44

idols—rejecting them as hero systems, sources of significance and meaning. In all this we are trying to trace out the psychological experience associated with the conflict Paul describes in Ephesians 6:12: "For our struggle is not against flesh and blood, but against the rulers, against the authorities, against the powers of this dark world and against the spiritual forces of evil in the heavenly realms."

Briefly stated, being set free from the slavery of the fear of death will necessitate a confrontation with the principalities and powers—a battle fought primarily around issues related to identity, self-esteem, and the pursuit of significance.

2.

A vast library of theological literature could be consulted to approach the biblical language of the principalities and powers, but for our purposes I'm going to draw on work that facilitates conversation with my discipline of psychology. This is not to dismiss other approaches. In the effort to build some preliminary bridges between theology and psychology, I'm opportunistically selecting locations where connections are obvious and straightforward.

Along these lines, we'll think of the principalities as suprahuman forces that exert a moral influence upon our lives. These forces are everywhere. I'm particularly fond of the approach and descriptions found in the work of William Stringfellow:

> According to the Bible, the principalities are legion in species, number, variety and name. They are designated by such multifarious titles as powers, virtues, thrones, authorities, dominions, demons, princes, strongholds, lords, angels, gods, elements, spirits. . . .
>
> . . . And if some of these seem quaint, transposed into contemporary language they lose quaintness and the principalities become recognizable and all too familiar: they include all institutions, all ideologies, all images, all movements, all causes, all corporations, all bureaucracies, all traditions, all methods and routines, all conglomerates, all races, all nations, all idols. Thus, the Pentagon or the Ford Motor Company or Harvard University or the Hudson Institute or Consolidated Edison or the Diners Club or the Olympics or the Methodist Church or

the Teamsters Union are principalities. So are capitalism, Mao-
ism, humanism, Mormonism, astrology, the Puritan work ethic,
science and scientism, white supremacy, patriotism, plus many,
many more—sports, sex, any profession or discipline, technology, money, the family—beyond any prospect of full enumera-
tion. The principalities and powers are legion.[1]

This list might seem strange and a bit of a stretch for some. How can
some of these things be classified as "spiritual powers"? For Stringfellow
this description is apt, since the institutions and ideologies he mentions
(and all others like them) exert a real moral force in our lives. We typically
experience this force as demands for our *service*, along with our moral and
spiritual *allegiance* and *loyalty*, which the Bible generally describes as idolatry. Stringfellow expounds on the pressures that the powers place upon us:

> [People] are veritably besieged, on all sides, at every moment
> simultaneously by these claims and strivings of the various
> powers each seeking to dominate, usurp, or take a person's
> time, attention, abilities, effort; each grasping at life itself; each
> demanding idolatrous service and loyalty. In such a tumult it
> becomes very difficult for a human being even to identify the
> idols that would possess him [or her]. . . .[2]

I think most of us have experienced what Stringfellow describes. In
our thirst for significance and meaning we often attach our lives to some
institution or cause. For example, I work at a university. As mentioned in
the last chapter, within the university (and feel free to imagine your own
place of work or the nation where you reside) there is a hero system, a way
to be recognized and noticed as a person of worth, value, and significance.
For the most part, this pathway toward recognition is associated with acts
of service to the institution, helping the institution accomplish its mission
statement. All of this service creates a flurry of activity. If your days are
anything like mine, they always include a mountain of work, deadlines, and
meetings. There are people below me to manage, managers above me to sat-
isfy, and a bottom line that calls for constant attention. And all of this work
creates the exact situation Stringfellow describes above, a situation in which
service to the institution threatens to "dominate, usurp, or take a person's
time, attention, abilities, effort." People feel harried, stressed, overworked,
and competitive. We become rivalrous with those *within* the institution and
combative with those *outside* the institution (e.g., other universities) who

---

1. Stringfellow, *Ethic for Christians*, 77–78.
2. Ibid., 90.

threaten and compete against us. And in all this we see how our own institution exerts a *moral* and *spiritual* influence, tempting us to put work before family or church or Christ. We are tempted to destroy rival institutions (or at least earnestly pray for their downfall). We are tempted to ignore moral imperatives if ever ethical scruples get in the way of accomplishing institutional objectives or hurt the bottom line. All of these examples can properly be described as idolatry.

So why do we do it? What do we get in return for all this work, stress, strain, and effort? We get the praise and approbation of the institution, which matters to us because as a suprahuman entity the institution seems more durable in the face of death. Likely the institution existed before we showed up, and likely it will exist after we die. My school is a relative youngster as far as American universities go, but it's been around for over a hundred years. And it might live on for a hundred more. Thus, by attaching myself to this institution—by making its life, mission, and values my life, mission, and values—I can obtain a sort of immortality, a sense that what I did with my life will last and endure. Here Stringfellow describes this temptation:

> Make work your monument, make it the reason for your life, and you will survive your death in some way. . . . Work is the common means by which [people] seek and hope to justify their existence while they are alive and to sustain their existence, in a fashion, after they die.[3]

The hope is that my contribution might "make a lasting difference" in the world. Thus, I become convinced that service to an institution marks a life well lived, a significant and meaningful life—a life immune to death.

And yet, we know this to be an illusion. Institutions regularly turn against those serving them. Sometimes people spend decades in faithful service only to be cut loose a year before retirement—no fanfare, no gold watch. Moreover, the seeming durability of institutions is a fiction. Institutions fail and nations fall. It's only a matter of time. We must remember that service to an institution, even when the soaring rhetoric of its mission statement suggests otherwise, provides no real protection from death.

Unfortunately, our fear of meaninglessness in the face of death is so great that despite all of the evidence, we continue to serve principalities and powers, hoping that because of their size, age, or power they will be able to save us. And the grip that these powers have upon us goes deeper than merely making us busy and stressed. As mentioned above, the real moral problem with our allegiance to the principalities and powers is how

---

3. Stringfellow, *Instead of Death*, 40.

the spirituality of these institutions and ideologies becomes internalized, becomes a form of "possession." In what follows I'd like to characterize this "possession" in more detail because the ultimate argument I want to make in this regard is that the spirituality we internalize when our self-esteem gets wrapped up in serving institutions or ideologies is the spirituality of death. I want to describe how these many forms of idolatry are ultimately involved in the worship of death and are thus another manifestation of our slavery to the fear of death.

3.

In what follows I'm going to lean heavily on the seminal work of Walter Wink regarding the principalities and powers.[4]

I will start by commenting on the biblical use of the phrase *archai kai exousiai*, which is often translated as "principalities and powers." This phrase occurs ten times in the New Testament. In the book of Luke, which contains the only occurrences of the phrase in the gospels, the pairing "principalities and powers" is used twice, and both instances refer to human political institutions:

> When you are brought before synagogues, rulers and authorities, do not worry about how you will defend yourselves or what you will say. . . (Luke 12:11)

> Keeping a close watch on him, they sent spies, who pretended to be honest. They hoped to catch Jesus in something he said so that they might hand him over to the power and authority of the governor. (Luke 20:20)

The other eight instances of *archai kai exousiai* occur in the epistles:

> Then the end will come, when he hands over the kingdom to God the Father after he has destroyed all dominion, authority and power. (1 Cor 15:24)

> For by him all things were created: things in heaven and on earth, visible and invisible, whether thrones or powers or rulers or authorities; all things were created by him and for him. (Col 1:16)

---

4. Specifically Wink's trilogy on the powers: *Naming the Powers* (1984), *Unmaking the Powers* (1986), and *Engaging the Powers* (1992).

... and you have been given fullness in Christ, who is the head over every power and authority. (Col 2:10)

And having disarmed the powers and authorities, he made a public spectacle of them, triumphing over them by the cross. (Col 2:15)

... far above all rule and authority, power and dominion, and every title that can be given, not only in the present age but also in the one to come. (Eph 1:21)

His intent was that now, through the church, the manifold wisdom of God should be made known to the rulers and authorities in the heavenly realms.... (Eph 3:10)

For our struggle is not against flesh and blood, but against the rulers, against the authorities, against the powers of this dark world and against the spiritual forces of evil in the heavenly realms. (Eph 6:12)

Remind the people to be subject to rulers and authorities, to be obedient, to be ready to do whatever is good.... (Titus 3:1)

Following Wink's lead, we can make a couple of observations about these passages. First, we see that there are times when the language of the powers seems to pick out strictly "spiritual" powers (e.g., Eph 6:12), and there are other times when the phrase picks out a strictly human, generally political power (e.g., Titus 3:1). But more often than not, the passages blend the two powers. For example, Colossians 1:16 clearly refers to both visible and invisible powers—powers in heaven and on earth.

The other thing to note is that the language of the powers often occurs in longer lists. As seen above, these lists include chief priests, rulers, people, scribes, synagogues, kingdoms, thrones, angels, authority, glory, majesty, dominion, life, and death. Such lists continue to highlight the conflation of physical and spiritual power in the New Testament.

The point here is that while there is a dualism at work in these biblical passages, it's not as dualistic as we might think. The regulating idea for the ancients seems to be this: manifestations of *physical* (generally *political*) power were manifestations of *spiritual* power. The two—physical power and spiritual power—were opposite sides of the same coin, intimately *connected*. And while this might seem strange, we can note that the ancients viewed their kings (political power) as divinities (spiritual/moral power). If the rulers were not fully divine, they were at least ordained by God (or the gods). To defy the king was to defy God.[5]

Now it is true that the ancients, given their cosmology, saw the spiritual powers as existing "over" or "above" the physical powers. This spatial orientation is hard for modern readers to get their heads around. In light of this, how might we preserve the tight association between the physical and spiritual powers?

Wink's suggestion is that we trade in the ancient above/below orientation for an inside/outside orientation. Rather than view the spiritual as "above" the physical, we can instead view the spiritual as the "inner" life—the "heart" and "soul," if you will—of a particular power structure or power relation (e.g., social, institutional, organizational, economic, national, political). For example, when we talk about a nation, an economy, an organization, or a corporation, we can consider the "spirituality" each embodies, the top-down culture and ethos that govern the lives of the individuals who serve and participate within those structures. By doing so, we might find a particular power structure to be, say, humane or inhumane. These descriptions pick out the "spirituality" of the power.

With this reframing in hand, Wink argues that we can continue to use the language of the satanic or the demonic to name the ruling ethos or spirituality of a power structure that is violent, degrading, and abusive. Below Wink describes how labels such as "demonic" or "satanic" name death-dealing spiritualities among the principalities and powers:

> What I propose is viewing the spiritual Powers not as separate heavenly or ethereal entities but as *the inner aspect of material or tangible manifestation of power.* . . . I suggest that . . . the "principalities and powers" are the inner or spiritual essence, or gestalt, of an institution or state or system; that the "demons" are the psychic or spiritual power emanated by organizations or individuals or subaspects of individuals whose energies are bent on overpowering others . . . and that "Satan" is the actual power that congeals around collective idolatry, injustice, or inhumanity, a power that increases or decreases according to the degree of collective refusal to choose higher values.[6]

5. And nothing much has changed. Before we consider the ancients superstitious and blinkered, we should note that we moderns similarly conflate the political and spiritual in how we sacralize the political realm. For us, God and country tend to be two sides of the same coin. Further, we also sacralize market economies, where the "invisible hand" is an all-knowing and benevolent god seeking our well-being. To question the "wisdom" of the market is to question a divinity. As it says on our currency: "In God we trust."

6. Wink, *Naming the Powers*, 104–5.

Now some might argue that if this is the case then the word *spirituality* isn't really necessary. But as we discussed in chapter 2, it is very difficult to physically locate these powers in the scientific laboratory. For example, the phrase "Give me liberty or give me death!" holds great power over many people and produces tangible effects upon the world. But where is that power physically located? In atoms? In the strong nuclear force?

My point is that the use of "spiritual" or "religious" language here isn't a regression into superstition. It is, rather, an attempt to describe how various supraphysical forces have power over human affairs. There are additional powers that are also hard to pin down in any scientific or reductionistic way, largely because they are distributed across space and time. On this point, Wink writes,

> Every organization is made up of humans who make its decisions and are responsible for its success or failure, but these institutions tend to have a suprahuman quality. Although created and staffed by humans, decisions are not made so much by people as for them, out of the logic of institutional life itself. And because the institution usually antedates and outlasts its employees, it develops and imposes a set of traditions, expectations, beliefs, and values on everyone in its employ. Usually unspoken, unacknowledged, and even unknown, this invisible, transcendent network of determinants constrains behavior far more rigidly than any printed set of rules could ever do. It governs dress, social class, life-expectations, even choice of marriage partner (or abstention). This institutional momentum through time and space perpetuates a self-image, a corporate personality, and an institutional spirit which the more discerning are able to grasp as a totality and weigh for its relative sickness or health.
>
> ... The *institution*, however, is the totality of its activities and as such is a mostly invisible object. When we confuse what the eye beholds with the totality, we commit the same reductionistic fallacy as those Colossians who mistook the basic elements (*stoicheia*) of things for the ultimate reality (Col. 2:8, 20). The consequence of such confusion is always slavery to the unseen power behind the visible elements: the spirituality of the institution or state or stone.[7]

The idea here is that a narrow and reductionistic focus on individuals fails to recognize the powers that operate in a more distributed fashion across time (often over the course of many human life spans) but that still exert a real causal influence on smaller scales. If that sounds complicated,

7. Ibid., 110.

consider hurricanes. By focusing on the physics that governs individual molecules, we miss the large-scale phenomena that organize all of those air molecules and create the event we know as a hurricane. In order to see and name the hurricane, we can't work at the level of individual air molecules. We need to step back and scale up, trading in a microscopic molecular picture for larger-scale macroscopic features like wind speed, temperature, humidity, and barometric pressure. We trade in atomic physics for the skills of the meteorologist. And if we want to know where the hurricane will come ashore, we'll rely on the skills of macroscopic description. In a similar way, the biblical language of the principalities and powers provides us with the skills of *macroscopic moral description*, allowing us to examine the moral forces within human affairs that can't be named by examining the behaviors and choices of isolated individuals.

4.

Here Wink and Stringfellow offer us some alternative language that can help us translate the biblical language of the principalities and powers into something more recognizable in our day-to-day lives. To be clear, I'm not saying that this is all that needs to be said or could be said about the principalities and powers. My interests here are fairly narrow and modest. My goal is simply to unpack the language of the principalities and powers in such a way that this language can pick out certain aspects of our experience. And my hope is that in making this connection, we will gain a clearer and more concrete understanding of what it means to say that "our battle is not against flesh and blood but against the principalities and powers" (Eph 6:12 NIV).

To summarize, then, our battle with the principalities and powers will tend to focus on resisting the spiritualities embodied in various power structures. As described by Wink above, the spirituality of a structure such as an institution, company, or nation can't be located in one particular place. Beyond artifacts (e.g., mission statements, policy and procedure manuals, founding documents), the spirituality of an institution is encoded across a variety of practices, beliefs, attitudes, habits, values, expectations, norms, and traditions. We become "possessed" by the principality and power when we internalize the spirituality of the system and the practices, beliefs, attitudes, habits, values, expectations, norms, and traditions *of the system* become the sources we use *to form our own identity*. And while the tag "possession" might seem extreme, it does help us name something more clearly, something left out of our descriptions at the start of the chapter regarding the ill effects associated with our service to the powers. Specifically, we previously noted how the powers can make us harried, stressed, and rivalrous. But it's a bit worse than all that. It's not just that the powers push us around from the *outside* with demands, deadlines, and expectations. The powers also affect (and infect) us from the *inside*. A focus on *service*—how we work and make sacrifices for the institution—tends to miss how we often *internalize the spirituality of the institution*, how our identity becomes formed by and fused with the institution. A focus on service and work (though important) tends to be too behavioral in nature to capture how the institution gets inside us, inhabiting our hearts and minds and affecting how we see ourselves, others, and the world around us.

As we explored above, we allow this to happen because we think that the durability of the institution makes it an existential lifeboat, a repository for our lives that will carry forward into the future long after we are gone. The allure of the principality and power is that it can do something that we cannot, namely, outlast death.

But as we noted, this is an illusion. Every institution, organization, and nation—every principality and power—plays the same game that we play, the game of survival and self-preservation. We know only too well that when the rubber meets the road the institution will do what it needs to do in order to survive. The "bottom line" (however that is defined) will have the final say. And this means that death—the ethos of the bottom line and the culture it creates—is as much at work with the principalities and powers as it is in our own lives. The death-driven spirituality of self-interest and self-preservation remains at the heart of it all. Yes, the principalities and powers offer us a route to success, self-esteem, and significance in exchange for a life of service. But this service is revealed to be idolatrous—a service rendered to death and aimed only at helping the institution survive. *Personal* self-preservation is simply being exchanged for *institutional* self-preservation. As Stringfellow describes it,

> The institutional principalities also make claims upon us for idolatrous commitment in that the moral principle which governs any institution—a great corporation, a government agency,

an ecclesiastical organization, a union, utility, or university—is its own survival. Everything else must finally be sacrificed to the cause of preserving the institution, and it is demanded of everyone who lives within its sphere of influence—officers, executives, employees, members, customers, and students—that they commit themselves to the service of that end, the survival of the institution.

This relentless demand of the institutional power is often presented in benign forms to a person under the guise that the bondage to the institution benefits the person in some way, but that does not make the demand any less dehumanizing. . . . In the end, the claim for service which an institution makes upon an individual is an invitation to surrender his or her life in order that the institution be preserved and prosper. It is an invitation to bondage.[8]

Thus, at the end of the day, the service we render to a principality and power, and any sense of esteem and significance derived from that service, is, at root, a service offered to death, the ethic of self-preservation and survival.[9] The neurotic pursuit of self-esteem via service to the powers is revealed to be another manifestation of our slavery to the fear of death. Thus is death found to be the Idol behind all idols, the great force sitting behind all the existential fetishes of success and significance proffered to us in the world by the powers. Stringfellow, once more, on this point:

Death is the only moral significance that a principality proffers human beings. That is to say, whatever intrinsic moral power is embodied in a principality—for a great corporation, profit, for example; or for a nation, hegemony; or for an ideology, conformity—that is sooner or later suspended by the greater moral power of death. Corporations die. Nations die. Ideologies die. Death survives them all. Death is— apart from God—the greatest moral power in this world, outlasting and subduing all other powers no matter how marvelous they may seem for the time being. This means, theologically speaking, that the object of allegiance and servitude, the real idol secreted within all

8. Stringfellow, *Free in Obedience*, 55–57.

9. Though my focus has been on work-related powers, the examples here could just as easily be focused on nations and political powers. Stringfellow once again: "Americans are now constantly, incessantly, and somewhat vehemently assailed with the word that the ultimate moral significance of their individual lives is embodied in and depends upon the mere survival of the American nation and its 'way of life' . . . [Consequently] the survival of the nation as such becomes the idol, the chief object of loyalty, service, and idolatry" (ibid., 58).

idolatries, the power above all principalities and powers—the idol of all idols—is death.[10]

In short, despite the shiny, heroic, and deathless allure of the principalities and powers, we can't escape death by serving them and sacrificing for them. Nor can we escape death by internalizing the spirituality of these powers. No matter where we turn in the world, the spirituality of death is all we will find. Death saturates our work, our worldview, our identity. Everything is held in bondage by our slavery to the fear of death.

10. Stringfellow, *Ethic for Christians*, 81.

PART 3

"There Is
No Fear in Love"

Chapter 5

An Eccentric Identity

1.

Our slavery to the fear of death compromises our ability to love each other fully, deeply, and sacrificially. So it's no surprise that 1 John claims that perfect love must cast out fear.

Here in Part 3, I want to describe what freedom from this bondage of fear might look like, psychologically speaking. What has to be accomplished in relation to our fear of death for love to flow forth freely and authentically?

2.

In Part 2 we discussed various aspects of our slavery to the fear of death and different expressions of our fear of death. Initially, we focused on more direct and conscious forms of this fear—what psychologists call basic anxiety, the inherent concern we all have for self-preservation that makes us naturally selfish. This issue of selfishness, which we'll soon discuss more thoroughly, isn't meant to be a harsh criticism, since this motivation is necessary for all biological creatures such as ourselves. For now, we simply note that this natural impulse toward self-preservation creates a moral bias within our hearts and minds, so that our focus is instinctively directed toward ourselves rather than toward others. Thus, in order to love we need to reverse this arrow, learning to say more often "no" to the self and "yes" to others. The problem here is that this switch is especially hard to make when we are anxious and fearful. For this reason, saying "yes" in love to others must involve managing the anxiety we feel when self-preservation isn't our number one priority.

3.

Beyond this sort of basic anxiety there are also neurotic forms of death anxiety that compromise our ability to love in three different ways. First, in affluent parts of the world neurotic anxiety, aided by technological advances and material wealth, has created cultures of death-denial and avoidance. Love becomes difficult in these cultures because expressions and signs of need are discouraged or hidden from view. And without authentic expressions of need, an economy of love, sacrifice, and care cannot take place. A society without need offers no occasions to serve each other or bear one another's burdens.

The second problem related to neurotic death anxiety is how our needs for self-preservation are sublimated as a desire for success and self-esteem. In affluent societies where self-preservation is not a pressing concern, we begin to worry about living a meaningful and significant life in the face of death. More specifically, in American society this anxiety tends to manifest in the American success ethos. That is, while we might not fear *death* on a day-to-day basis, we do fear being a *failure* in the eyes of others (or ourselves). But failure here is simply a neurotic manifestation of death anxiety, the fear that at the moment of death we won't have accomplished enough to have made a permanent and lasting difference in the world.

The most common route toward making such a difference is to become beholden to the principalities and powers. We receive affirmation from these powers. For most of us this affirmation involves the praise and successes that we experience in our workplaces, though we should also consider other forms like national pride and flag-waving patriotism. This affirmation is a ready-made route to daily self-esteem, significance, the feeling that we "matter." In addition, as suprahuman entities, the powers seem more durable and immune to the ravages of death—immortal even. Isn't America the *Eternal* City? Won't America be around *forever*?

All of this interferes with our ability to love because our drive to be a "success," which is often defined by the principality and power we serve, becomes so all-consuming that it absorbs all our time, energy, and attention—valuable resources that could be devoted to loving others more fully. To be clear, we all need to work, and there is nothing immoral about taking care of our basic biological needs. What I am critiquing here is when our thirst for "success" becomes a form of demonic possession, an all-consuming passion where the next achievement or conquest pushes aside concern and care for others. If we are to love each other fully, we must be able to say "no" to the principalities and powers in order to say "yes" to others. In other words, we must be willing to sacrifice priorities like personal "success" and "significance" in order to love. Concretely, think of the person who turns down a promotion at work because the new position would compromise his or her ability to be present to family, friends, church, or neighborhood. And yet, few of us make these sorts of decisions, because we are bound by neurotic anxiety. Turning down a promotion means facing a flood of neurotic anxiety, being perceived (now and in the future) as a failure or loser who couldn't keep up. Turning down a promotion means enduring the neurotic anxiety of disappointing the institution, an institution that makes our life meaningful and significant.[1] It's hard to turn away from the principalities and powers because serving them feels so good, so rewarding, so intoxicating, so essential. It feels great to be recognized as successful, indispensable, and valuable.

And yet, it's a trap. As we noted in Part 2, the principalities and powers are not immortal. Moreover, the ethos of self-preservation rules the spirituality of the powers as surely as it rules our own lives. Putting in a sixty-hour workweek won't make our lives matter any more than if we turn down the promotion. Some of us learn this lesson the hard way when a corporation downsizes and we are let go. Some of us learn when a company fails or is exposed as morally corrupt and spiritually dead. Some of us learn only at the end of life, looking back on all of our sacrifice—a lifetime of neglecting loved ones and lives of service in order to serve a principality—and wondering, "What was it all for?" Unfortunately, many never learn the lesson at all.

---

1. This is no hyperbole. Even if we hate our job, merely having one is a source of self-esteem. Just ask the unemployed about how being jobless affects self-image and social shaming. Having a job is a foundational aspect of the American cultural hero system.

4.

This is such an important point I'd like to linger and dig a little deeper here, as it is very hard for many of us to detect how our slavery to death manifests in how our culture and workplaces manipulate our self-esteem in demanding greater and greater allegiance, service, and sacrifice. Again, recalling our discussions from Part 2, it's not that the principalities and powers bully us into dumb servitude. Rather what happens is that we internalize—willingly, even cheerfully—the *spirituality of the institution*. And what is so hard for many of us to see is how the spirituality of the institution is actually a manifestation of our slavery to the fear of death.

So let me dig a little deeper here. Let's look behind the language of "excellence" in the workplace.

In the language of the psychologist Barry Schwartz, I tend to be a satisficer rather than a maximizer when it comes to things like work. That is, I tend to aim for "good enough" rather than "excellence" or "the best." But this tendency of mine sets me at odds with the zeitgeist of our age—the pursuit of excellence, of being the best—particularly in the world of corporate America.

But deep below the surface the motive behind the "pursuit of excellence" is a neurotic fear of death that plays upon our insecurities at being "normal" or "average" or merely "good enough." The powers then use the language of "excellence" to exploit these neurotic anxieties, using these fears as leverage in demanding greater and greater sacrifices for the institution or organization.

But there is a lie at the root of the language of excellence. The lie is that excellence—striving to be the best, or even merely better—assumes that we are gods, creatures immune to death. Excellence assumes that we are not, in fact, finite creatures with finite resources of time and energy. More technically, the narrative of excellence is supported by a false—and neurotically delusional—anthropology.

Of course, let me add, a lot depends here upon one's definition of excellence. By excellence I'm pointing to the impulse in our culture where being satisfied with being "average" or "normal" or "good enough" is somehow an admission of defeat or failure, a giving up or a throwing in the towel. By excellence I'm pointing to the neurotic drivenness that demands constant improvement, that this year—personally or institutionally—has to be better than last year.

But as should be clear, this is impossible. You can't get better and better and better. Again, we are not gods with infinite resources. We are finite, limited creatures. We have a ceiling, a limit. Past a certain point, you can't get better.

That is, unless, you start borrowing—or robbing—from other facets of your life. You *can* get better at work if you begin to borrow some time or energy from, say, your family. To get better at work you can work longer hours by spending less time elsewhere. Because this is the only way a finite creature can get better. Not being a god you can't tap into an infinitely deep reservoir of time and energy. You have to borrow from somewhere to get ahead elsewhere.

In this we see how excellence presupposes a false anthropology that assumes that we are gods and not human beings. Human beings, of necessity, have to be "good enough." Or, at the very least, *excellence entails sacrifice*—borrowing from one aspect of life to get ahead in another area. Sacrifice-free excellence is unavailable to us. We are not gods.

This is why cultural and workplace calls for "excellence"—calls for ever escalating betterment, progress, and improvement—are really, at root, *a demand for more sacrifice*, for greater allegiance, service, and loyalty to the institution, organization, or nation. Of course I could do "better" in various areas of my life. I could throw in more time, energy, or resources. But if I do so, what will I have to sacrifice?

To give an example from my own professional life, there are a variety of areas at work in which I've achieved a "good enough" level. But my workplace doesn't want "good enough"; it wants excellence and constant improvement. Being "good enough" is an admission of failure, and the workplace culture (along with the overarching American culture) is set up to make me keenly experience this failure through shame and social comparison. We should strive to be the best. Or, at the very least, we should be better than we were last year. And even better next year, and the year after that, and so on. Eternal improvement is the name of the game.[2]

But again, this is impossible. The only way I can improve and improve and improve is if I start, say, taking time away from my family or church. Excellence is here revealed to be a euphemism for sacrifice and idolatry. Yes, I could be a *better* worker—but at the expense of being a *worse* father, spouse, or friend.

And yet—and this is the critical point—most of us are ready and willing to make these sacrifices. We buy into the illusion and the lie. We don't want to "settle" for being good enough, so we neurotically pursue excellence

---

2. Otherwise what? Otherwise you *die*. You have to keep improving and improving or you'll die, institutionally. Once again we see how death drives the culture and ethic of the powers.

and betterment. As discussed in Part 2, we internalize the spirituality of the powers.

And why do we do this?

It goes back to our slavery to the fear of death.

Again, being "average" or "good enough" is generally experienced as a form of failure. But this neurotic feeling of failure is really just masking a deeper anxiety. As we've just diagnosed the situation—being "good enough" isn't about our *failure* as much as it is about our *finitude*, our being mortal creatures. This is where the fear of death enters in. Being "average" or merely "good enough" provokes existential anxiety as we are confronted with our limitations. Again, there is a delusional anthropology behind the quest for excellence. We'd like to think that we have *inexhaustible resources*—all the time and energy in the world—to be excellent in *everything*. Which is to say we'd like to be gods, creatures immune to death. This desire to be godlike—to be excellent—is driven by a fear of our own mortality, a fear of facing our own finitude and limitations. Failure—not being excellent—reminds us that we are humans and not gods, that we are mortal creatures vulnerable to death. And this is a realization we'd rather avoid.

And so our discomfort with our failures and our discomfort with being "average" or "normal" or "good enough" is revealed to be another manifestation of our slavery to the fear of death. The neurotic push for excellence—a spirituality of our culture and workplaces that we internalize—is found to be driven by a fear of death, a fear that is regularly exploited by the principalities and powers to draw time, energy, and resources away from loving others.

Wanting to be excellent is wanting to be immune from death, to be immortal, to become a god. And this delusion can be maintained, but only at the expense of others.

5.

And finally, beyond hiding our need and neurotically pursuing self-esteem, there is a third way our neurotic anxiety about death interferes with love. And this is the darkest manifestation of all, as it makes us violent.

Because our worldview is the source of our significance and self-esteem, we want to defend it from the criticisms of out-group members. Those who are different from us implicitly or explicitly call into question the things we hold most dear, the cultural values that ground and shape the contours of our identity and self-esteem in the face of death. In this, out-group members become a source of anxiety, an existential threat. To cope with the anxiety, we rush to defend our worldview and become dogmatic, fundamentalist, and ideological in regard to our values, culture, and way of life. We embrace our worldview as unique and exceptional, as superior to other worldviews, which we deem inferior, mistaken, and even dangerous. This mindset begins the process in which out-group members are denigrated and eventually demonized, sowing the seeds of violence. The point to note here is how this violence is fueled by an underlying neurotic fear that the cultural projects that we've invested in and sacrificed for are not actually immortal, eternal, timeless, or immune to death.

6.

Such are the consequences of our slavery to the fear of death.

So the question becomes, what needs to happen to replace all this anxiety with love? How do we acquire the courage to turn away from our innate inclination toward selfishness and instead attend to the needs of others? How can we come to endure the shame of rejecting a culture of death avoidance in choosing to authentically and transparently expose our needs and weaknesses to others? How do we fight off the fever of success in order to experience what appears to be failure in the eyes of the principalities and powers? How can we come to reject fear and death and embrace love and life?

How do we experience the liberation of Christus Victor that empowers us to say "no" to the works of the devil and "yes" to Christ?

In this and the chapters that follow I will argue that this courage comes from two places—the formation of a new sort of *identity* and the formation of a new sort of *community*. In this chapter and the next we'll talk about a new identity, then in chapter seven we'll turn to issues of community.

7.

I argued in Part 2 that our slavery to the fear of death goes deep. This anxiety doesn't simply concern basic survival fears; rather, it goes to the roots of our identity, saturating everything that seems to make our life significant and meaningful. And if this is the case, being set free from the slavery of death requires a complete overhaul of our identities. In the language of Paul, the "old man" will have to die so that a "new creation" can be raised to take its place. Liberation from the slavery of death involves death and resurrection.

Let's first try to describe the identity that must be put to death so that we might better discern the shape of our new identity in Christ.

I'd like to start by returning to the work of Arthur McGill, who shares some potent insights about the particular sort of courage required by love. According to McGill, the courage involved in love manifests in how we approach our own neediness. But his point here is actually a bit more sharp—and scary—than my description above. McGill argues that true love not only involves being more comfortable *revealing* our needs to others, but it also *moves us into a state of neediness*. Love *creates* need in our lives. Consequently, we are unable to move into this state of neediness, into love, if we are anxious about death—fearful of need, loss, failure, weakness, and diminishment. Because of this connection between need and love, a failure to embrace our need, a failure driven by fear, will compromise our ability to meet others with empathy and compassion in the midst of their own need. McGill explains:

> [The love that is proclaimed in many churches] carefully disregards the outcome of love. These churches speak of love as helping others, but they ignore what helping others does to the person who loves. They ignore the fact that love is self-expenditure, a real expending, a real losing, a real deterioration of the self.
>
> . . . Too often in our churches we hear the gospel of love without the gospel of need. Too often we hear the lie that to love is to help others without this help having any effect upon ourselves.[3]

The point here is that love involves sacrifice, that love is costly. And while this may seem banal and obvious, McGill's argument is that many Christians think that loving others can be done in such a way that love will have no real impact upon their lives. Love, as many Christians seem to conceive of it, costs nothing and requires no real sacrifice. We can see the neurotic death-denial at work here, creating and maintaining the fantasy that we can always say "yes" to ourselves and simultaneously "yes" to everyone else. Need, want, and lack don't exist in this illusion of deathlessness.

But need really does exist, and sacrificial love will quickly bring it to the surface. We find that when we give, what we give isn't always replenished. This truth is what marks love as love, as something more than mere exchange, as an act of grace. The account books are not balanced. Love gives gifts and makes sacrifices and expects nothing in return.

3. McGill, *Death and Life*, 87–88, 90.

And yet, our natural inclination is to experience anxiety in the face of all this. When our actions become costly, when the sacrifices get too big, our natural worries over self-preservation begin to kick in. If I continue to love, if I continue to give, what is going to happen to me? As Jean Vanier, founder of L'Arche, observes, "People are sometimes frightened of following Jesus because they are frightened of *losing* things."[4]

All this points to the tension between the fear of death and the call to love, illuminating how the two are always pitted against each other. The fear of *losing* pitted against the call of *giving*. Thus love, of necessity, involves facing down this fear. Love is an act of *courage* in the face of death. McGill comments, "The only love that has anything to do with Jesus Christ is a love that has no fear of need, of neediness, of poverty."[5]

According to McGill, our fear of need, loss, failure, and diminishment (our fear of death) has caused us to configure our identities in a particular way. He calls this an "identity of possession"—an identity of ownership, territoriality, and proprietorship—and he believes it is constructed in one of two ways:

> First, I may try to seize bits of the world for myself. Second, I may act in such a way that I will be approved by other persons or forces so that, in reward for something I have done or because they expect themselves to benefit from me, they will deliver some bit of reality over into my control.[6]

McGill labels these two routes to identity *aggression* and *appeasement*. The former strategy roughly corresponds to our discussions about basic anxiety, the Hobbesian situation where we act suspiciously and aggressively to protect what we possess from the claims of others. The latter strategy parallels our discussions of neurotic anxiety and how we try to please the principalities and powers. Both strategies are attempts to create and form an identity by possessing something. I am who I am because of what I own or control. Very often these possessions are material, like income and all that it can purchase. But many of these possessions are more social and symbolic in nature, and they serve more neurotic ends like securing the respect of others through titles, positions, influence, reputation, or status. Regardless, an identity built upon possession—material or social—is vulnerable to the forces of death. Such an identity crackles with fear, infused with worries over loss, failure, diminishment, and dispossession. These anxieties will

4. Vanier, *Community and Growth*, 137.

5. McGill, *Death and Life*, 90.

6. Ibid., 53.

inevitably produce the sinful outcomes we discussed in previous chapters. As McGill writes,

> [When we define our identity] in terms of a reality which we can have and which we can securely label with our own name, we live under the dominion of death; we live under the dominion of dispossession. We live in terror of death, of having this bit of reality which we call ourselves, taken from us. Our whole existence is controlled by that terror.[7]

Love is impossible when we build our identities in this manner because this terror becomes the controlling force in our lives and our sense of self becomes enslaved to the fear of death.

So how, then, are we set free from this slavery? The identity of possession must "die" and an altogether different sort of identity must be "raised to life" in its place. We hear an echo of this in Jesus' words from the Sermon on the Mount:

> Do not store up for yourselves treasures on earth, where moth and rust destroy, and where thieves break in and steal. But store up for yourselves treasures in heaven, where moth and rust do not destroy and where thieves do not break in and steal. For where your treasure is, there your heart will be also. (Matt 6:19–21 NIV)

While some might read this exhortation as an argument for otherworldliness, our analysis suggests another interpretation. Jesus' focus here is on the heart and where it is located, and he speaks about how *the location of our identity makes it more or less susceptible to damage and loss.* An identity built around the notion of possession—built around "treasures on earth"—is vulnerable to the power of death. Consequently, our lives become dominated by fear and worry. Jesus confirms this analysis by quickly shifting his Sermon into his great discourse about fear:

> Therefore I tell you, do not worry about your life, what you will eat or drink; or about your body, what you will wear. Is not life more than food, and the body more than clothes? Look at the birds of the air; they do not sow or reap or store away in barns, and yet your heavenly Father feeds them. Are you not much more valuable than they? Can any one of you by worrying add a single hour to your life?
>
> And why do you worry about clothes? See how the flowers of the field grow. They do not labor or spin. Yet I tell you that

7. Ibid., 54.

not even Solomon in all his splendor was dressed like one of these. If that is how God clothes the grass of the field, which is here today and tomorrow is thrown into the fire, will he not much more clothe you—you of little faith? So do not worry, saying, "What shall we eat?" or "What shall we drink?" or "What shall we wear?" For the pagans run after all these things, and your heavenly Father knows that you need them. But seek first his kingdom and his righteousness, and all these things will be given to you as well. Therefore do not worry about tomorrow, for tomorrow will worry about itself. Each day has enough trouble of its own.

These are challenging words, but I think our focus on identity is helpful here. I don't think Jesus is criticizing our efforts to care for our basic needs and the needs of our loved ones. Rather, he seems concerned about a fear-driven identity, about the location of the heart and its susceptibility to damage and how this vulnerability infuses our identities with anxiety. He knows that a heart located "on earth" will be preoccupied with gathering, securing, and protecting, and he understands that the worries associated with these efforts make us competitive, rivalrous, envious, acquisitive, and aggressive. According to Jesus, the antidote for this sort of existence is storing up treasures "in heaven," where death has no dominion. But what might that look like?

Let's return to McGill's analysis. If an identity of possession is driven by a fear that produces sinful outcomes, what sort of identity should take its place? McGill looks for clues by closely examining the identity of Jesus in the gospels. Where does Jesus get his identity? What is it based on (how is it formed)? And how does Jesus' identity differ from our identity of possession? According to McGill, the key notion is this: Jesus doesn't possess his identity. Rather, Jesus has what McGill calls an "ecstatic identity," an identity that is not *owned* but received as a *gift*:

> In the New Testament portrayal of Jesus, nothing is more striking than the lack of interest in Jesus' own personality. His teachings and miracles, the response of the crowd and the hostility of the authorities, his dying and his resurrection—these are not read as windows in Jesus' own experience, feelings, insights, and

growth. In other words, the center of Jesus' reality is not within Jesus himself. Everything that happens to him, everything that is done by him, including his death, is displaced to another context and is thereby reinterpreted. However, this portrayal is understood to be a true reflection of Jesus' own way of existing. He himself does not live out of himself. He lives, so to speak, from beyond himself. Jesus does not confront his followers as a center which reveals himself. He confronts them as always revealing what is beyond him. In that sense Jesus lives what I call an ecstatic identity.

In all the early testimony to Jesus, this particular characteristic is identified with the fact that Jesus knows that his reality comes from God. . . . Jesus never has his own being; he is continually receiving it. . . . He is only as one who keeps receiving himself from God.[8]

McGill argues that the key to Jesus' identity is that he doesn't "possess" it, but instead *receives* it as a *gift*. The center of Jesus' identity exists *outside* of himself. In the language of David Kelsey, Jesus is living an "eccentric existence" that we are all called to adopt and emulate. Kelsey describes this eccentric, outside-of-self orientation in this way:

The question "Who are we as creatures?" makes it clear that while I have my personal identity only in and through relations with other creatures of giving and receiving, my personal identity is not given to me by them in their assessment of me and does not depend on their judgments of me. My personal identity is free of them, grounded elsewhere. I am radically given to directly only by the triune God. Faith as trust responsive to God's giving is the attitude that my right to be and act, and the justification of the time and space I take up being and acting, is not contingent on my meeting the needs or acquiring the approval of any of those finite others to whom I give and from whom I receive in the society of creatures. Faith is the attitude of trust in God's radical giving of reality as alone definitive of my personal identity: a finite creature called and empowered to be, to act, and to give in my own place and time. Your personal identity is defined by God alone and not by any creature. It is eccentrically grounded and defined.[9]

An "eccentric" identity is an identity grounded *outside* the boundary of the self. An eccentric identity, thus, is the opposite of McGill's identity of

---

8. McGill, *Death and Life*, 49–50.

9. Kelsey, *Eccentric Existence*, 339–40.

possession where, as he describes it, "I have a boundary which marks the domain of my reality."[10] As McGill observes, Jesus did not define his identity in this manner, but rather had an "ecstatic" or "eccentric" identity[11]—one found outside of himself and grounded in the Father. Jesus' treasures, to borrow from the Sermon on the Mount, were stored up in heaven. Consequently, Jesus was not motivated by the fears, worries, and neuroses that motivate us. Jesus feared nothing. He was competitive with no one, aggressive toward no one. And why? Because Jesus' identity was formed in a way that liberated him from the slavery to the fear of death. Consequently, in the words of Chrysostom from Part 1, Jesus was free from the tyranny of the devil. Because Jesus didn't own himself, he could not be dispossessed of himself. The fear and neuroses that push and pull our identities had no effect upon Jesus, and thus he was free to love spontaneously and generously. We see from Jesus' example how the eccentric identity makes love possible. McGill explains the dynamics of this Christlike, eccentric identity and illustrates how it overcomes the predicaments we've described in the previous chapters:

> Because I no longer live by virtue of the reality which I possess, which I hold, which I master and keep at my disposal, I am free to share myself and all my possessions with others. Above all . . . I can be honest with others. I can be open before them. I do not have to draw a line to mark the boundaries of my reality where I place a sign which says "Keep Out." I do not have to conceal my being behind a wall in order to keep it mine and to prevent others from taking it from me. Since I never have myself, I can never be dispossessed of myself. In short, in all my relations with other people I am freed from the anxiety of having always to keep possession of my own reality in order to be.[12]

8.

I'd like to pause and spend a little more time here trying to describe the psychology associated with an eccentric identity, an identity found and rooted in God, an identity emancipated from the slavery of death. I think

10. McGill, *Death and Life*, 53.

11. McGill's term is "ecstatic identity," but going forward I'll be using Kelsey's term, "eccentric identity," as the word *eccentric* so nicely captures, in its fusion of geometrical and normative allusions, how the Christian identity is located beyond and outside the boundaries of the self and how an identity so formed is rare, atypical, and unusual.

12. Ibid., 51–52.

such a psychological description would be helpful as it will allow us to make diagnostic judgments as to how we might discern when the eccentric identity has been strongly established and how we might know when our emancipation from the slavery of death is being realized within our own lived experience.

Again, when our identities become eccentrically grounded, they are found in God, a location where they cannot be damaged or lost. And because of this, fear is replaced with a sense of peace.

What might that feel like? I'm reminded here of the analysis of Howard Thurman in his book *Jesus and the Disinherited*—a book, it is said, that Martin Luther King Jr. carried with him wherever he went. Writing about the black experience in the Jim Crow South, Thurman seeks to articulate the power of the gospel for those "who stand, at a moment in human history, with their backs against the wall."[13] According to Thurman, for those with their backs against the wall the gospel provides "profound succor and strength to enable them to live in the present with dignity and creativity."[14] Given our focus on the experience of an eccentric identity, an identity received from God, Thurman's analysis is of interest. In the Jim Crow South the principalities and powers were antagonistically arrayed against the black population. Socially, politically, and economically marginalized, there was little in the hero system of the South that gave support to black identity and self-esteem. To psychologically survive in this milieu, blacks of necessity had to develop an eccentric identity, an identity found *outside* of the hero system of the surrounding Jim Crow culture. In that setting, Thurman argues, the gospel provided Southern blacks with a grounding for self-identity and dignity. He writes:

> The core of the analysis of Jesus is that man is a child of God. . . . This idea—that God is mindful of the individual—is of tremendous import. . . . In this world the socially disadvantaged man is constantly given a negative answer to the most important personal questions upon which mental health depends: "Who am I? What am I?"
>
> The first question has to do with a basic self-estimate, a profound sense of belonging, of counting. If a man feels that he does not belong in a way in which it is perfectly normal for others to belong, then he develops a deep sense of insecurity. When this happens to a person, it provides the basic material for what the psychologist calls the inferiority complex. It is quite possible for a man to have no sense of personal inferiority as such, but at

13. Thurman, *Jesus and the Disinherited*, 11.
14. Ibid.

the same time to be dogged by a sense of social inferiority. The
awareness of being a child of God tends to stabilize the ego and
results in a new courage, fearlessness, and power. I have seen it
happen again and again.[15]

Of psychological interest here is how an identity rooted in the grace of
God—an identity eccentrically grounded in God—stabilizes the ego in the
face of social shaming, hostility, and violence. This resiliency in the face of
social shaming and hostility will be an important focus in the next chapter
when we discuss the psychological and social conflicts involved in renouncing our allegiances to the principalities and powers. For now we simply note
how an eccentric identity rooted in the experience of knowing oneself to
be beloved by God provides a rock-solid grounding for self-worth: "a basic
self-estimate, a profound sense of belonging, of counting." Moreover, as described by Thurman, this experience of "belonging" and "counting" in the
eyes of God inoculates the ego in the face of fear:

> [Seeing oneself as a child God establishes] the ground of per-
> sonal dignity, so that a profound sense of personal worth can ab-
> sorb the fear reaction. This alone is not enough, but without it,
> nothing else is of value. The first task is to get the self immunized
> against the most radical results of the threat of violence. When
> this is accomplished, relaxation takes the place of churning fear.
> The individual now feels that he counts, that he belongs.[16]

Obviously, Thurman is describing here the threats of physical violence
that were the daily reality of blacks in the Jim Crow South. In light of this,
I want to be clear that I am not comparing my experience, or the experience of any other white person in America, with the experiences of black
Americans in the Jim Crow South. I want to focus not on the social reality
Thurman is describing but on his psychological analysis; he is describing
a psychological experience that I think gets at the root of what happens
when fear has been lifted from the spirit and soul, what it feels like to be
set free from the slavery of death. As Thurman describes it, the eccentric
identity— "the ground of personal dignity . . . a profound sense of personal
worth" that comes to us when we receive our identities as children of God—
immunizes the self from "churning fear." Anxiety is replaced by a state of
relaxation. And this relaxation—grounded in the fact that the "individual
now feels that he counts, that he belongs"—inoculates the ego from fear.

15. Ibid., 49–50.
16. Ibid., 50.

This relaxation comes from the "awareness of being a child of God," which stabilizes the ego and "results in a new courage, fearlessness, and power."

Overall, I would argue that this experience of feeling beloved as a child of God, along with the accompanying experience of relaxation, even in the face of both psychological and physical threat, is diagnostic of the eccentric identity. Some people might, for biblical or theological reasons, prefer the word *peace* over *relaxation*,[17] but I like the word *relaxation*. It highlights the body and points to how our fear response, and the peace we are speaking of, is embodied. And that is helpful for diagnostic purposes. People can say they are at peace when you can see in their body that they are angry, agitated, or anxious.

Experiencing, in the face of whatever life throws at us, a feeling of relaxation—real physiological relaxation, rooted in knowing that we are beloved of God: this is, in my estimation, a key sign that the eccentric identity has firmly taken root.

9.

Before concluding our discussion of the eccentric identity, I'd like to make one more biblical connection.

This notion of the eccentric identity sits very close to the biblical notion of kenosis, the *emptying* of the self. Note how in Philippians 2 Paul describes Jesus' personality as a contrast between kenosis and "grasping," an almost exact parallel with our descriptions of the eccentric identity and the identity of possession:

> Do nothing out of selfish ambition or vain conceit. Rather, in humility value others above yourselves, not looking to your own interests but each of you to the interests of the others.
>
> In your relationships with one another, have the same mindset as Christ Jesus:
> Who, being in very nature God,
>   did not consider equality with God something to be used
>   to his own advantage;
> rather, he made himself nothing
>   by taking the very nature of a servant,
>   being made in human likeness.
> And being found in appearance as a man,
>   he humbled himself
>   by becoming obedient to death—

---

17. And in chapter 7 we'll be speaking of joy.

even death on a cross! (Phil 2:3–8)

Paul points to the eccentric, kenotic identity of Jesus as the solution to the problems of love in the Philippian church. The Christians in Philippi were operating out of an identity of possession, an identity characterized by grasping and clinging. They were motivated by "selfish ambition" and "vain conceit." Note their desire to possess—their impulse to hold onto status, influence, esteem, reputation, and power—and how it became their route toward self-definition, self-esteem, personhood, and identity.

As a remedy Paul points to Jesus' eccentric and kenotic identity, helping the Philippians see how Jesus did not operate out of an identity rooted in grasping, owning, and possessing. Because Jesus did not have to anxiously defend against the claims or encroachments of others, he was able to truly let go and love. He could empty himself (kenosis) for the sake of others. And because Jesus did not fear dispossession or loss, he could endure the social and cultural stigma of being "nothing." Jesus was able to carry the burden of shame—a burden that, due to his identity, must have seemed very light—of being the lowest on the social ladder, a servant to all, one of "the least of these." To use terms from the American success ethos, Jesus did not fear looking like a failure or a loser—he did not worry about humiliation. Jesus was free from every form of death anxiety, both basic and neurotic. Again, this freedom was the outcome of Jesus' eccentric identity, which Paul describes as the engine that empowered Jesus to live a life of love and sacrificial other-orientedness. Consequently, Paul asks his readers to adopt this same eccentric identity—to have "the same mindset as Christ Jesus"—so that they too will be able to "look to the interests of others." And again, referring back to Howard Thurman's analysis, the courage and capacity that makes kenosis possible—the inoculation of the ego that is required to endure shame, loss, perceived failure, and all other forms of "emptying"—is the foundational conviction that we count and matter, that we are the beloved children of God. Only when the ego has been stabilized in this manner can we turn toward others with relaxed, non-grasping, and other-oriented love.

Chapter 6

The Sign of the Cross

1.

Throughout the New Testament our identity in Christ is described as being created by a sort of death. I hinted at this at the end of the preceding chapter by connecting the eccentric identity with kenosis. In Philippians 2 the outcome of Jesus' self-emptying—the endpoint of his eccentric orientation—is the cross. The cross thus becomes a multivalent symbol. On the one hand it is a sign of physical death, but it also represents another sort of death: kenosis, the continual practice of self-emptying and servanthood that leads to a final sacrifice. Thus, beyond being a sign of *death*, the cross also becomes a sign of *love*, of the willingness to give one's entire life away for the sake of others. In this, the cross becomes the logical endpoint of the eccentric identity. When our identities are rooted in God, we cling to nothing and thus have the psychological capacity to make sacrifices for the sake of others. Jesus interprets his cross for his disciples in this way, teaching them that it represents love and self-expenditure for the sake of others:

> Greater love has no one than this: to lay down one's life for one's friends. (John 15:13)

In other words, the cross symbolizes the Christian identity and the call to willingly "lay down our lives" for others.

This is how we know what love is: Jesus Christ laid down his
life for us. And we ought to lay down our lives for our brothers.
(1 John 3:16)

As Arthur McGill succinctly notes, "The way of Jesus is the way of self-
expenditure."[1] And as Paul describes in Philippians 2, this freedom to give
our lives away is made possible only through the act of kenosis, of self-emptying and letting go so that our identities might be eccentrically grounded
in Christ and the Father. If we receive everything—even our very lives—as
a gift, then we have nothing to cling to or to protect. Following the example
of Jesus, we become "nothing." In a sense, we "die"—and thus we no longer
have to fear dispossession, loss, diminishment, or expenditure in the face
of death. Not that we seek out such losses.[2] But we form our identities in
such a way that we are freed from the anxiety of self-preservation, which
makes different choices and modes of being human open and available to
us. The creation of a secure heart makes love a possibility. It enables us to do
something that biological creatures worried about self-preservation don't
naturally do: place the interests of others before our own.

This capacity is created when we become indifferent to the anxiety that
arises when we begin to act lovingly, when we begin to put ourselves at the
end of the line and allow others to go before us. We become indifferent to
the basic anxiety attendant to acts of material sacrifice for others, as well
as to the neurotic anxiety attendant when we forgo success (as our culture
defines it) and place ourselves in the role of servant. In both instances, this
indifference is symptomatic of a sort of death and signals that certain vital
concerns no longer animate us, no longer give us life. The spirituality of
death that had previously possessed our beings has been "exorcised" and
replaced with the animating and life-giving Spirit of Jesus. The cross represents this death, a death that points to a kenotic indifference that creates the
space and capacity to love. This is a death that brings about the possibility
of resurrection.

2.

But my hunch here is that all this discussion about radical self-expenditure,
about laying down our lives and taking up the cross, is making some of us
anxious and likely causing some of us to hesitate. What am I asking us to
do—lay down our lives and become martyrs?

1. McGill, *Death and Life*, 81.
2. More on that in the next chapter.

In a sense, yes.

What tends to happen when we talk about carrying the cross of Jesus is that we get distracted with heroic visions of "laying down our lives for others" and miss how all this plays out in more mundane circumstances. For example, let's revisit 1 John 3:16 and also look at the following verse. Note the concrete expression of "laying down" one's life:

> This is how we know what love is: Jesus Christ laid down his life for us. And we ought to lay down our lives for our brothers. If anyone has material possession and sees his brother in need but has no pity on him, how can the love of God be in him? (1 John 3:16–17)

Here the martyological ideal—that Jesus Christ laid down his life for us, and thus we ought to lay down our lives—isn't connected to something heroic but to something simple and fairly unexciting: generously sharing, caring, empathizing, and giving. And what this suggests is that there is no *qualitative* distinction between the martyr and the Christian in everyday life. The distinction is only *quantitative*, a difference not of kind but of degree.

This is the argument Craig Hovey makes in his book *To Share in the Body*. Hovey argues that, while it is true that in the face of, say, state-sanctioned persecution, Christian martyrdom may involve dying for the faith, this heroic ideal misses the point that martyrdom is the calling of every Christian. As Dietrich Bonhoeffer famously said, "When Christ calls a man, he bids him come and die."[3] For Hovey, martyrdom is less about being burned at the stake on some foreign mission field than it is about the *small daily acts of self-expenditure and self-donation that we make in order to love and serve others*. Martyrdom, according to Hovey, is best displayed in small acts of *asceticism*, moments of self-denial in which I say no to the self in order to say yes to the needs and claims of others. He explains:

> *Askesis* (from which *asceticism* is derived) is a term that names the training or discipline of self-denial. . . . In the same way, martyrdom names not an ethic but an effect or outcome of the *askesis* of one's whole life, one's needs, and the way of life that would meet them. . . . The way of Jesus requires the unseating of those modes of behavior, ways of life, desires, and thoughts that are conditioned on scales of self-preservation, self-protection, and security for one's life. . . . The virtues necessary to be a martyr are no different from the virtues necessary to be a faithful Christian. This means that martyrdom is not a special calling

---

3. Bonhoeffer, *Cost of Discipleship*, 89.

for a select few but the commitment of every Christian and the responsibility of every church.[4]

We are well positioned to hear the point Hovey is making. Martyrdom is *a discipline of daily living* that renounces "modes of behavior, ways of life, desires, and thoughts that are conditioned on scales of self-preservation, self-protection, and security for one's life." These are the modes of life that are driven by our slavery to the fear of death. At the end of the day, the martyrs show us that being non-anxious in the face of death frees us to make mainly small, but even large, sacrifices for others. If the martyrs are a witness to anything—martyr simply means "witness"—it is to freedom from fear in the face of death. By emulating Jesus, each martyr proves that liberation from slavery to the fear of death and "the tyranny of the devil" is possible. Hovey emphasizes that this freedom is what should characterize everyday Christian living. Rather than being held in reserve for some heroic sacrifice, our kenotic indifference to "looking toward our own interests" (a focus driven by basic and neurotic forms of death anxiety) needs to be displayed throughout our lives in small steps of courage and routine acts of daily self-expenditure. This is the pattern we see in 1 John 3:16–17, in which simple acts of *sharing* are found to be a form of *martyrological witnessing*, a real expression of "laying down our lives" as Christ did for us.

Sharing is a *cruciform* and *martyrological* act because, as we noted in the last chapter, true sharing will move us into a state of need. Consequently, sharing, as with all forms of sacrificial giving, will be infused with an anxiety that is rooted in our slavery to the fear of death. Thus, the self-renunciation involved in carrying our crosses is also inherently involved in overcoming our fears of death—fears, as Hovey noted, that are rooted in concerns over "self-preservation, self-protection, and security for one's life."

3.

The cross, then, is a symbol of self-denial and renunciation. Under the sign of the cross we undergo a sort of death so that we might become immune to the power of death. Jesus himself places self-denial at the heart of the cross:

> Then Jesus said to his disciples, "If anyone would come after me, he must deny himself and take up his cross and follow me. For whoever wants to save his life will lose it, but whoever loses his life for me will find it. What good will it be for a man if he gains the whole world, yet forfeits his soul?" (Matt 16:24–26b)

4. Hovey, *To Share in the Body*, 59–60.

Here Jesus points to a self-denial of a particular sort. He describes an asceticism that rejects a certain mode of being, which we've already named the "identity of possession." In Philippians 2, Paul describes the rejection of this identity as an act of kenosis, and above Jesus speaks of "losing." Both terms target an identity grounded in possessing. Jesus rejects an identity grounded in "gaining," and Paul rejects an identity rooted in "grasping." Salvation is found in *losing* (to use Jesus' term) and *emptying* (to use Paul's), both pointing to a *death* that leads to *life*. This, as we've repeatedly noted, is an inversion of how we typically approach the world. Driven by our anxieties regarding self-preservation, we tend to think *gaining and grasping are the routes to securing life*, and as biological creatures—as *sarx,* to use Paul's language—it is natural to think this way. But as we came to see in Part 2, an identity built around this impulse is an identity founded upon death and enslaved to the fear of death. Thus, the paradox of the cross: we must *die*—by losing and letting go—in order to find *life*, in order to experience resurrection.

4.

Of course, the great sign of this dying to the powers of sin, death, and the devil and then being raised to a new life in Christ is the ritual of baptism. In baptism we "die" to an old mode of being, a death that we've described above as inherently an act of renunciation. Following Jesus' call to lose our lives and Paul's appeal to empty ourselves, we renounce the parts of our identities that give the devil moral traction, the parts that are fearful and anxious in the face of death and thus keep us bound to sinful practices. From the baptismal vows included in the *Book of Common Prayer*:

> Do you renounce Satan and all the spiritual forces of wickedness that rebel against God?
>
> *I renounce them.*
>
> Do you renounce the evil powers of this world which corrupt and destroy the creatures of God?
>
> *I renounce them.*
>
> Do you renounce all sinful desires that draw you from the love of God?
>
> *I renounce them.*[5]

---

5. *Book of Common Prayer,* 302.

The Christus Victor themes are fully evident here. Baptism is a renunciation of Satan, sin, and the evil powers at work in our hearts and minds. But many Christians have a thin view of what this renunciation looks like—we tend to think of it as an act of willpower, as simply resisting cravings and temptations. This perspective is symptomatic of the Protestant focus on piety; however, the Christus Victor frame we've explored in earlier chapters shows that the problem is much deeper and more pervasive. Sin, in this view, is less about hedonic *craving* than it is about our *slavery* and *bondage*. The issue isn't *temptation* as much as it is *identity* and how we ground our sense of self-definition and self-worth. So, as I've tried to describe above, our baptismal renunciations are less focused on willpower (i.e., saying "no" to temptation) and more concerned with a deep reconfiguration of our personhoods.

Of interest here is how Craig Hovey describes this "switching of identities" in baptism as a changing of *allegiances* and a transfer from one kingdom to another:

> In baptism, a human individual is transferred from the world to the church. The world registers a loss in loyalty; the church registers an advance in loyalty. . . . Because of this shift, baptism marks a definite realignment of power. . . . If the church grows through the initiation of one member at a time, it seemingly shrinks through an equivalent but opposite process. The world attempts to regain its lost members, to secure its former loyalties, and to establish its earlier power. In this way, baptism is an overtly political act. Like the burning of draft cards, baptism declares a switched identity, a refusal to be one thing and a determination to be something else.[6]

Hovey's image of baptism being akin to a political act, the burning of draft cards, is striking. This observation allows us to bring in other parts of our discussion from Part 2 and to highlight another important aspect of the cross: how the cross serves as a sign of antagonism toward the principalities and powers.

This focus is important as most of our discussion to this point regarding the eccentric identity and the daily martyrdom of self-denial has focused upon the basic anxieties associated with our impulse toward self-preservation. For example, above we talked about sharing and how when we let go of material possessions we experience anxiety about having "enough" for ourselves. We have yet to fully discuss how the eccentric existence of Jesus addresses the more neurotic manifestations of our slavery to death. That is to say, being able to "lay down our lives" for others involves more

6. Hovey, *To Share in the Body*, 32–33.

than becoming relaxed and non-anxious when we are asked to share material goods. There is more to martyrdom than mere physical courage. As we undergo small and large acts of self-giving and self-expenditure, there are neurotic anxieties that must also be faced.

Hebrews 12 clearly signals that, more than physical courage, this way of life involves "fixing our eyes on Jesus, the pioneer and perfecter of faith."

> For the joy set before him he endured the cross, scorning its shame, and sat down at the right hand of the throne of God. Consider him who endured such opposition from sinners, so that you will not grow weary and lose heart. (Heb 12:2–3)

Jesus' courage here is framed as a victory over *neurotic* anxieties. What Jesus scorns is not the physical pain of the cross but the *shame*, the *humiliation* of the cross. The writer of Hebrews uses the cross of Jesus to encourage his readers to endure their own "opposition from sinners," their own social shaming and humiliation.

When we change allegiances in baptism, we are renouncing the way the world defines significance and value. Concretely, the hero systems found in serving the principalities and powers offer a vision of "success," a vision that guides just about everyone around us. These hero systems set the rules of the game by which winners and losers, successes and failures, are defined. We gain self-esteem—a sense of accomplishment and significance—by trying to win this game and earn as many blue ribbons as possible. But in baptism, Christians turn their backs on this game, return the blue ribbons, and reject the things that give others value, respect, and significance. By this act, Christians register a dissent that implicitly indicts how everyone else is choosing to live their lives. And we can't kick out the props of everyone else's self-esteem without expecting a negative response. When we scorn the blue ribbons that make everyone else feel important, we are going to face some backlash. Moreover, the systems of the world aren't able to function if people stop chasing those blue ribbons, so the principalities and powers will eventually push back. Thus, we observe the antagonism between Christians and the powers that begins with baptism.

The courage here, then, becomes less about maintaining our physical well-being (the concern we might have with sacrificial sharing and giving) than about being non-anxious in facing the shame that accompanies the social and institutional pushback. That is, carrying the shame of the cross involves being set free from the neurotic fears of looking like a failure to those around us. The cross doesn't just represent physical courage in the face of death; it also represents the courage to look foolish to friends, family, coworkers, and the world at large. This foolishness is less about excessive sharing—although that's a part of it—and more about returning our blue ribbons in order to play another sort of game.

Paul speaks to this foolishness, this appearing "out of our mind," in 2 Corinthians:

> If we are "out of our mind," as some say, it is for God; if we are in our right mind, it is for you. For Christ's love compels us, because we are convinced that one died for all, and therefore all died. And he died for all, that those who live should no longer live for themselves but for him who died for them and was raised again.
>
> So from now on we regard no one from a worldly point of view. Though we once regarded Christ in this way, we do so no longer. Therefore, if anyone is in Christ, the new creation has come: The old has gone, the new is here! (2 Cor 5:13–17)

This text weaves together many of the themes we've discussed. We see the eccentric identity on display: we do not hold on to ourselves, drawing boundaries around the self that must be defended against the needs and demands of others. Rather, we are eccentrically found "in Christ." Further, this change of identity is experienced as a death and a resurrection. The old has gone and a new creation is raised to take its place. The concrete expression of this identity is that "we regard no one from a worldly point of view." We reject the hero system of the world and replace it with a new vision of success and failure, and in doing so we appear to be "out of our minds."

Paul's own biography is a wonderful illustration of this journey. He describes his death in Jesus as a *loss*. A loss of what? A loss of *identity*. Or more precisely, a loss that involved rejecting the way in which he had *built* and *grounded* his identity. Paul died to the hero system of his culture and to all the blue ribbons he had gathered while living and succeeding within that system. For Paul, "death" in baptism meant that he counted as "rubbish" his accomplishments within that hero system:

> But whatever was to my profit I now consider loss for the sake of Christ. What is more, I consider everything a loss compared to the surpassing greatness of knowing Christ Jesus my Lord, for whose sake I have lost all things. I consider them rubbish, that I might gain Christ . . . (Phil 3:7–8)

Note the relationship between self-esteem and the identity of possession. What Paul considered "profits" were the accomplishments that had given his life meaning and significance in his eyes and the eyes of his culture. Within his culture's hero system, Paul *mattered*. But this sense of self-esteem, as we discussed in Part 2, made Paul a slave to sin and death. We should also note here how Paul's sense of *significance*, rooted as it was in neurotic anxiety, made him *violent*, a persecutor of the church. This is exactly what Ernest Becker described—how we protect our hero systems against out-group members. And for Paul, being a Jew, this protection included persecuting Christians. Paul's violence was driven by his thirst for self-esteem.

But in baptism Paul rejects the identity of possession by counting his prior heroics as *loss*: "I consider *everything* a *loss*." Paul no longer owns anything. And Paul's assessment here is less about his material position in the world than it is about his *psychological ownership of his former heroic accomplishments*, the blue ribbons that he used to collect to make himself "matter" in the face of death. Paul empties himself of all these accomplishments and, following the example of Jesus in Philippians 2, no longer considers these accomplishments things worth clinging to or grasping at. Instead, Paul renounces them as "rubbish" and exchanges his identity of possession for an eccentric identity of only "knowing Christ." Christ becomes Paul's one and only possession. Or rather, by possessing nothing, Paul becomes able to be possessed by Christ, held by and found in Christ. And because of this, death loses its power over Paul. Paul experiences resurrection; Paul is set free.

5.

To step into this freedom is to step into a place where death has lost its power. This is why death in Christ brings about resurrection, the ongoing event in our lives in which death has no dominion. Our victory over death is something that happens before physical death, a victory found in the capacity to experience life in this moment, emancipated from slavery to the fear of death. Resurrection in Christ, then, becomes freedom from death's power in daily existence. William Stringfellow describes resurrection this way:

> Resurrection . . . refers to the transcendence of the power of death and the fear or thrall of the power of death, here and now, in this life, in this world. Resurrection, thus, has to do with life and, indeed, the fulfillment of life *before* death.[7]

Again, Stringfellow:

> [Christ's] power over death is effective not just at the terminal point of a person's life but throughout one's life, during *this* life in *this* world, right now. . . . His resurrection means the possibility

---

7. Stringfellow, *Simplicity of Faith*, 138.

of living in this life, in the very midst of death's works, safe and free from death.[8]

The promise here is that, no matter what awaits us at the moment of death, in this moment and in every moment we can experience resurrection, our lives liberated from the slavery of death. Through this resurrection, we are no longer self-interested survival machines driven by fear, pushed and pulled by our survival instincts. Neither are we neurotically chasing an illusory vision of "success" as an attempt to matter in the face of death. Rather, by dispossessing ourselves in baptism, by denying ourselves and taking up the cross of Jesus, we ground our identities in Christ alone and count everything else as "rubbish." And in doing this—in dying to the world—death loses its hold on us, loses its moral traction to scare or shame us. Death has been defeated in the midst of our lives and Jesus' resurrected life becomes tangibly present within our own. Slavery to the fear of death has been exchanged for the freedom and capacity to love.

8. Stringfellow, *Free in Obedience*, 72.

Interlude

Timor Mortis

1.

Before moving on to the final chapters, I'd like to pause and address a few potential objections to the analyses offered in the last two chapters.

Specifically, is it healthy to be fearless in the face of death?

My discussion of martyrs here might have pushed some buttons in this regard—particularly in an age of religiously motivated terrorism and suicide bombers.

I offer two responses.

First, fearlessness is not an end in itself, but a means toward an end—love. The goal isn't simply to *be* courageous, the goal is a courage *for*. This is a courage that has love and other-orientedness as its *telos*, its endpoint, its goal. The point here is that our fear of death is the primary obstacle to love. Consequently, this fear must be overcome if we are to love others sacrificially through acts of self-giving and self-donation. I am not advocating a fearlessness that valorizes an indifference to life that manifests itself in violence, destruction, or nihilism. Neither do I deny the fact that fearlessness in the face of death might be pursued for those sorts of ends. So, the issue is a matter of motivation and the goal for which one is cultivating courage.

This brings us to a second set of questions: can the fear of death truly be eradicated and, if so, would that be psychologically healthy? To answer, I'd like to return to the issue of martyrdom and journey with St. Augustine, exploring the development of his thoughts about *timor mortis*.

2.

Timor mortis is Latin for the "fear of death" (*timor* being the root of *timorous*, and *mortis* the root of *mortality*). *Timor mortis* has an interesting history in the thought of Augustine, and tracing the development of his thought can help us address questions about psychological well-being and fearlessness in the face of death. Further, Augustine helps us ask some other significant questions. Does the faithful Christian *never* fear death? Is the fear of death a sign of spiritual cowardice and a lack of faith?

3.

In his early writings Augustine does seem to suggest that Christians should not fear death. To fear death would be a sign that the Christian did not trust in God and the resurrection. Here Augustine seems to have been greatly influenced by the heroic feats of both pagan and early Christian martyrs, individuals who showed no fear in facing death. For Augustine this martyrological ideal seems to be the standard he felt Christians should aspire to. In addition, Augustine was also influenced by the Stoics, who argued that the truly wise and virtuous would be calm and fearless in the face of death. Exemplars here are Socrates and Seneca.

This heroic ideal sets before us an almost impossible standard. Normal people do fear death. Does this mean that we lack faith? Does it mean that we remain enslaved by the fear of death?

4.

Over time, however, Augustine began to moderate his stance on *timor mortis*. His early treatments of the issue may have been overly influenced by his desire to place the courage of Christian martyrs on the same heroic level as the pagan heroes, philosophers, warriors, and martyrs who faced death with valiant scorn or philosophical indifference. In this, Augustine was writing early on in a vein more apologetical than pastoral, defending the faith against criticisms of inferiority (e.g., a Christian losing heart in the face of death wasn't a very inspirational vision compared to, say, Socrates calmly drinking hemlock). Later, as Augustine's interests in *timor mortis* become more pastoral, we find him backing away from the heroic ideal of the Christian martyr scorning death.

This change in Augustine's views regarding *timor mortis* started during the Pelagian controversies.[1] We need not unpack why those specific controversies sparked such a change, but let us simply note that as a result of the conflicts Augustine began to take a more realistic stance about Christians' experience of *timor mortis*. Crucially, he came to believe that *timor mortis* was not indicative of a spiritual or moral failure, and he eventually argued that the fear of death is a natural, regularly occurring feature of being human. Consequently, the goal of the Christian life is not to eradicate *timor mortis* but to *master* it when it interferes with the purposes of the Kingdom of God. The virtue here is less about scorning death than about daily fortitude and perseverance in the face of ever-present anxieties about death. Carole Straw summarizes this development of Augustine's viewpoint:

> Before Augustine, conquest of the fear of death was held to test the faith of Christians in the immortality of the soul and the resurrection; it proved confidence in the reward awaiting a life of virtue. Fear of death revealed doubt, guilt, and a misguided attachment to the body. Augustine began his career within this tradition, but the controversies he faced led him to change his views. . . . [As a result of the Pelagian controversies] Augustine will come to reject the triumphalism of earlier tradition. He will accept fear of death as a part of the human condition. Fear of death is a natural response that does not indicate want of faith; rather, it affirms the value of bodily existence realized finally in the resurrection. Prudence also dictates that one fear death to check sinfulness.[2]

Various arguments seem to have moved Augustine in this direction. First, he comes to realize that a complete absence of *timor mortis* causes Christians to become indifferent to issues such as suicide. In fact, an absence of *timor mortis* might even cause some Christians to use suicide as a sign of faith. That is, if *timor mortis* is a lack of faith in the resurrection, wouldn't suicide become the ultimate expression of faith? Augustine senses this line of argument and works hard to push back. For example, in the *City of God* he mentions the student of Plato who, upon reading about the immortality of the soul, got up and jumped off a building to his death. Isn't that faith? If so, is that the sort of faith and fearlessness the Christian should display?

---

1. For a summary of this development, see Dodaro, *Christ and the Just Society in the Thought of Augustine* (chs. 2 and 3 in particular).

2. Straw, "*Timor Mortis*," 838.

Augustine realizes that a line of reasoning similar to the one followed by Plato's student could be worked out from within the Christian faith. Specifically, why should we struggle with the Christian life when we could simply commit suicide after being baptized? Wouldn't suicide be the easiest and safest way to guarantee our salvation? Augustine floats this argument:

> [W]hy do we spend time on those exhortations to the newly baptized. [sic] We do our best to kindle their resolve to preserve their virginal purity, or to remain continent in widowhood, or to remain faithful to their marriage vows. But there is available an excellent short cut which avoids any danger of sinning; if we can persuade them to rush to a self-inflicted death immediately upon receiving remission of sins, we shall send them to the Lord in the purest and soundest condition![3]

To this Augustine responds, "if anyone thinks that we should go in for persuasion on these lines, I should not call him silly, but quite crazy"—and he concluded that "suicide is monstrous."[4]

But why? For Augustine faith isn't really faith until it has wrestled with the fear of death across the life span. That is, a lack of concern about death isn't a sign of faith. Rather, faith is manifested in the daily wrestling *with* death, which is what perfects faith over time. As Augustine says, our faith doesn't mean "that death had turned into a good thing."[5] No, he contends, "the death of the body . . . is not good for anyone."[6] So the goal of the Christian life is not to seek out death or to treat life cheaply. Death is evil and we are to struggle against death and resist all of its manifestations. This struggle implies that life is worth preserving, and this valuing of life always introduces anxiety. So the fear of death is simply an acknowledgment of the gift and goodness of life itself. To be indifferent to our lives would be to spurn the gift of God. *Timor mortis*—wanting to preserve our own lives—is, at root, an act of gratitude.

What we see in all this is how love, given the preciousness of life, will always be operating with a backdrop of anxiety. *Timor mortis* functions as the requisite testing ground of love. And according to Augustine, the constant fight to choose love over *timor mortis* "increases the merit of patience if it is endured with devout faith."[7]

---

3. Augustine, *City of God*, 1.27 (Bettenson, 38).

4. Ibid., 1.27 (Bettenson, 38–39).

5. Ibid., 13.4 (Bettenson, 514).

6. Ibid., 13.6 (Bettenson, 515).

7. Ibid.

5.

In summary, *timor mortis* is a fact of life and a regular feature of the Christian experience. The fear of death is always with us, moment by moment and day by day, and its absence would signal an indifference that could be, by turns, pathological, triumphalistic, or a spurning of the gift of life. The fearlessness we should seek is not an emotional blankness in the face of death. Such a blankness would be unable to make a distinction between life and death, and thus would be an act of ingratitude to God for the gift and goodness of life. Rather, the fearlessness we are speaking of involves an *overcoming* rather than a numbness, a refusal to let death be *the motive force* in our decision-making and identity formation. The fear of death remains, as both a temptation and a reminder of the gift of life, but it is given no dominion. And this is less about a once-and-for-all heroic decision than it is a daily act of obedience, perseverance, and sacrifice. The key point is that as biological creatures, our natural instincts toward self-preservation and survival cannot be wholly eradicated. If they were, a host of psychological and social ills would soon follow. These instincts point to the intrinsic value and goodness of life, as well as to the God-given imperative to cherish and protect both our own lives and the lives of others. And yet we are easily tempted to cherish our own lives above all others, which makes love impossible. The problem is that life, though originally given as a gift, becomes a location of possession and ownership. When this happens gratitude for the gift of life gives way to survival fears, and the cherishing of life gives way to suspicion and aggression.

In short, the way of the cross isn't about eradicating our biological instincts, but about learning to master them and creating the capacity to love without having our existence reduced to a Darwinian matrix. We might say that the way of the cross is about animals—*sarx*—learning to become both human and humane.

But for that to happen, death and its attendant anxieties cannot be the ruling power and spirituality of our lives. As biological creatures, we are not saved from the *fear* of death—that would be an impossible, foolish goal. We are, rather, saved from a *slavery* to the fear of death. When perfect love casts out fear, it does not fully eradicate the fear of death, but it empowers us to deny the *dominion* of death and gain victory over the *moral power and influence* of death in our lives. Across the great spectrum of fear—from merely feeling foolish in the eyes of others, all the way to mortal terror—the cross grants us the ability to choose love instead of death.

Chapter 7

───── ∞∞∞ ─────

Practicing
Resurrection

1.

Love is possible only when we've been set free from our slavery to the fear of death. Love necessarily involves mastering anxieties that are natural to biological creatures such as ourselves, because while these anxieties signal the goodness and preciousness of life, when left unchecked they produce a variety of sinful outcomes. If expressed directly, these survival anxieties can reduce human existence to a Hobbesian and Darwinian struggle, a perpetual state of anxiety, vigilance, suspicion, paranoia, rivalry, envy, competition, and aggression toward others. On the other hand, if sublimated, these anxieties produce a neurotic death avoidance that drives the quest for significance, meaning, and self-esteem. This quest, fueled by an underlying anxiety, produces similar forms of rivalry, competition, and aggression as we compete with others for attention, respect, and significance. Our neurotic fear of failure creates an inauthentic and appearance-obsessed social world, and our pursuit of self-esteem and significance typically leads us to serve (and seek the adulation of) the institutions around us—the principalities and powers. But upon inspection, and particularly when the powers treat us as disposable, we come to see that our survival fears contaminate any significance we gain from the powers, as well as our identities.

In sum, our anxiety in the face of death creates either *suspicion* or *superficiality* depending upon whether our anxiety is basic or neurotic, whether we are focused on *survival* or *self-esteem*. Either way, love becomes compromised in the face of these fears.

To be set free from these dynamics—to be liberated from slavery to the fear of death—we need to create a new sort of identity. As described in chapters 5 and 6, this new identity is an eccentric identity, one received as gift rather than owned as a possession. Such an identity allows us to engage in acts of kenosis—letting go of the self in order to expend ourselves (even to the point of death) on behalf of others. Not needing to own, protect, or defend the self frees us to donate ourselves in love. William Stringfellow admirably summarizes this entire argument in his book *A Private and Public Faith*:

> The power to discern God's presence in common life is imparted when one becomes a Christian, an event in which the power of the Word of God in one's own personal history is manifest over and over against the power of death. Then and thereafter the Christian lives in any and all events in reliance upon the presence of the Word of God. Then and thereafter the Christian lives to confront others, whatever their afflictions, with the news of God's care for the world. Then and thereafter the threat of our own eventual historic death holds no fear for us, for there is nothing which we will on that day experience which we have not already foretasted in the event of becoming a Christian, in the event of our surrender to the power of death and of our being saved from that power by the presence of God. Then and thereafter we are free from the most elementary and universal bondage of humanity: the struggle to maintain and preserve, whatever the cost, our own existence against that of all others. Then and thereafter are we free to give our present life away, since our life is secure in the life of God.[1]

The act of being a Christian is an eccentric reliance upon the Word of God "against the power of death." As discussed in chapter 6, this eccentric reliance represents a death as we come to depend no longer upon ourselves or upon the principalities and powers. In baptism we extract our egos from these supports, severing their power to infuse our lives with anxiety. To borrow the words of Stringfellow, we become "free from the most elementary and universal bondage of humanity: the struggle to maintain and preserve, whatever the cost, our own existence against that of all others." And this

---

1. Stringfellow, *Private and Public Faith*, 66.

freedom makes us "free to give our present life away, since our life is secure in the life of God."

With this vision in mind, I'd like to use this chapter to share some reflections about how we might create and sustain this eccentric reliance upon God that undergirds the capacity to give our lives away for the sake of the world. How are we to cultivate within our lives—both individually and collectively—what Stringfellow describes as "the genius of the Christian life"? Stringfellow writes, "[T]he genius of the Christian life, both for a person and for the company of Christians, is the freedom constantly to be engaged in giving up its own life in order to give the world new life."[2]

For biologically and neurotically self-conscious creatures such as us, this sort of freedom is not natural. Such a life—learning to give your life away—takes extensive training. But although unnatural, Stanley Hauerwas describes this training as the process of learning to "become a human being":

> To learn to follow Jesus is the training necessary to become a human being. To be a human being is not a natural condition, but requires training. The kind of training required, moreover, has everything to do with death. To follow Jesus is to go with him to Jerusalem where he will be crucified. To follow Jesus, therefore, is to undergo a training that refuses to let death, even death at the hands of enemies, determine the shape of our living.[3]

In this chapter I'd like to offer a preliminary sketch of what this training might look like.

2.

Before beginning a discussion of practices, let us consider a few concrete examples of both the eccentric orientation and the capacity to love that it creates. Our discussions in chapters 5 and 6 were fairly abstract and theoretical in nature, so these real-life examples may help bolster our understanding. With these pictures in mind (along with any others you can think of) our discussion of practices will be more focused. My hope is to show how some particular practices might shape our identities in such a way that we can love others more fully.

Our first picture comes from a scene in *Of Gods and Men*, a movie based upon the true story of nine Trappist monks who lived in the monastery

2. Ibid., 78.

3. Hauerwas, *Working With Words*, 78

of Tibhirine in Algeria.[4] In 1996 seven of these monks were kidnapped and killed by Islamist rebels during the Algerian civil war. In the years before the war, the monks lived peacefully among the residents of Tibhirine and were devotedly serving their Muslim neighbors. During the hostilities, which started in 1991, the monks faced mounting danger as radical Islamic groups begin to persecute and kill Christians in Algeria. Because the monks rejected government protection, they became increasingly vulnerable to a violent raid as the hostilities intensified in the area. And as these dangers increased, the monks were confronted with a choice: to leave the country or to stay and continue their ministry. Although leaving the country would have been the prudent course of action, the monks of Tibhirine refused to abandon their friends and neighbors but elected to stay and continue caring for the sick and the poor. This choice proved fatal when, on the night of March 26, 1996, seven of the monks were captured and killed by rebels.

Most of the movie is a meditation upon the choice that the monks faced: will they abandon Tibhirine for the sake of self-preservation and survival, or will they reconcile themselves to the prospect of death and continue to serve the town? In short, *Of Gods and Men* is a meditation on the central theme of this book. Which force will have the final say in the monks' decision—fear or love?

One scene, a microcosm of the whole film, captures just about everything I've tried to communicate in this book. In this scene, Luc, the monastery doctor who is the embodiment of the spiritual heart of both the monastery and the town, is talking with Christian, the leader of the monastery. Luc has been treating some of the Islamic rebels injured during the war—men who may eventually (and ultimately do) kill the monks. Christian warns Luc to be careful in treating these men, and Luc responds with words that capture and crystallize the themes of this book:

CHRISTIAN: *Be careful.*

LUC: *Throughout my career I've met all sorts of different people. Including Nazis. And even the devil.*

(pause)

I'm not scared of terrorists, even less of the army. And I'm not scared of death.

I'm a free man.

---

4. For a good historical treatment, see John Kiser's *Monks of Tibhirine: Faith, Love, and Terror in Algeria.*

Luc is able to love his enemies and the people of Tibhirine because he is "a free man," liberated from slavery to the fear of death. Note that Christus Victor themes are also present in Luc's mention of the devil. And the point here is that while Luc isn't entirely fearless, he *does not allow fear to have the final and ultimate say in how he makes his decisions.* Love leads the way and takes its place in the calculus of Luc's life. Love can be his choice. Even in the face of death, Luc is a free man.

Our second picture comes from William Stringfellow's *My People Is the Enemy*, a memoir of the time he spent living as a lawyer in a Harlem slum during the 1960s. Stringfellow recounts the life and death of his friend Lou Marsh, a black man who worked with gangs in New York. When trying to negotiate a truce between two rival gangs, Marsh was beaten to death by gang members who resented his pacifistic interventions. In the book Stringfellow describes Marsh's spiritual journey and explained how he unexpectedly came to work among violent gangs in New York. Though Marsh grew up in a poor family, his intelligence and sensitive spirit enabled him to pursue higher education and become a seminarian at Yale, which is where he and Stringfellow met. But something went wrong. According to Stringfellow, Marsh was filled with self-loathing for being a black man trying to accommodate himself to white society. Perhaps he felt guilt and shame for having escaped the poverty that still plagued his family and the rest of black America in the sixties. After leaving New Haven, Marsh descended into depression and began to drift, unemployed, dependent on handouts, and sleeping on friends' couches. At times Marsh slept on the streets, and eventually the self-loathing reached the point where he became suicidal. It was there, when he couldn't go any lower, that Marsh experienced a conversion. Stringfellow describes the event as follows:

> That was the moment—when Lou was in Hell—in which he knew, I think for the first time, that he was loved by God. That was the event in which by the power of God in the face of the fullness of death, Lou was emancipated—set free to love himself, to love others, and to welcome and receive the love of others. That was the time of Lou's salvation, the time of his reconciliation with himself and with the rest of the world.
>
> What followed was more or less predictable. Having been so intimate with the presence of death in his own life, but having beheld the reality and vitality of the Resurrection in his own life in the same event, Lou was free to live for others.
>
> So that is what he did.[5]

---

5. Stringfellow, *My People Is the Enemy*, 146.

Marsh's experience of resurrection freed him to love others. According to Stringfellow, he was liberated from the fear of death, which allowed him to pour his life into the lives of the troubled and violent youth of New York. Having been freed by love from his fear of death, Lou Marsh was no longer anxious about his own life or the risks associated with the work he was doing. Stringfellow continues:

> [Lou] took this job with the Youth Board and soon was so pre-occupied in caring for the kids in his gang that he forgot himself, so fulfilled in his love for others that he lost his self-interest, so confident that he was now secure in God's Word that he was not afraid of death.
>
> He was no longer afraid to die the way he died. He knew about the real risks of his job, especially the way he was now free to do his job. The way he died was surely no surprise to Lou. Not that he sought such a death, or any sort of death, any longer, but he was ready to die and was without fear of death. He no longer was in bondage to the alienation of men from each other. . . .[Lou] had become so free he could give away his own life freely—and surely that is the secret of reconciliation in Christ.
>
> Lou Marsh, when he died, was ready; that is, he had already died in Christ and so was without fear of death. That is the freedom the resurrection bestows upon men.
>
> That is the only way to die, which at the same time means that this is the only way to live.[6]

The biography of Lou Marsh—his life, conversion, ministry, and death—gives us a flesh-and-blood picture of what resurrection looks like: liberation from the slavery of death. Note how Marsh's new identity was eccentric and kenotic in nature. As Stringfellow explains, because Marsh became secure in God's love, he "forgot himself" and "lost his self-interest," which allowed him to love others. Liberated from the fear of death, Lou Marsh "had become so free he could give his own life freely."

The stories of Lou Marsh and of the monks of Tibhirine can be described as heroic stories, even martyr stories. They are the stories of persons who came to be so liberated from the fear of death that they were able to make loving choices that placed their physical lives in danger. Liberated from the fear of death, both Lou Marsh and the monks were truly free to transcend anxious self-interest and to share their lives fully with others. They were free, in short, to love. Perfect love had cast out fear. Lou Marsh

---

6. Ibid., 146–47.

and the monks of Tibhirine took up the cross of Jesus, laying down their lives for others in love. In this, their stories represent the final outworking of the logic of Christian love, the full manifestation of the martyrological identity described in chapter 6. However, we might quail in the face of these stories, so let me reemphasize my previous point that there is no real difference between the choices made by the monks and Lou Marsh and those made every day by ordinary Christians. While there may be a difference of *degree*, there is no difference of *kind*. Across the board—from soccer mom to the martyr—we all face the same choice: whether or not to say no to death and yes to love. Recall Craig Hovey's observation from chapter 6: "The virtues necessary to be a martyr are no different from the virtues necessary to be a faithful Christian."[7] The virtues in question here focus on a simple dynamic: allowing the self to experience diminishment for the sake of others. As Arthur McGill points out, love always involves diminishment, loss and a "casting out fear" in the face of that loss.

So lest we despair that the bar is being set too high, let us pause to consider a less heroic example: Jesus' admonition in Luke 10:14 to "take the lowest place" in social situations. When we engage in this seemingly innocuous action, real diminishment takes place. For example, forgoing opportunities to "sell" or "promote" ourselves in the workplace and choosing, instead, to point out others' good work often has real consequences in the business world. We like to think that good, honest work will be recognized in the long run, but that is not necessarily the case. Thus, being able to "take the lowest place" in life requires us to master the neurotic anxiety that we might get "passed over," that we might not "get ahead" or be as "successful" as others. If we don't master this fear we begin to anxiously push, overly asserting or promoting ourselves in an attempt to claim the "first place." In this our identity becomes shaped by *possession*, the desire to claim and own the first place against the claims of others.

The point here is that simple acts of humility in the workplace can have real effects on our lives. Even if these effects aren't directly economic, "taking the last place" involves a loss to the ego. Since we all want respect and recognition, forgoing praise involves a real loss to the self. Again, nothing in these sorts of daily choices is qualitatively different from the choices of the Christian martyrs. Christian love will always have this martyrological character—a willingness to undergo a "death" in order to give life to others.

Upon reflection, we all know this to be true. Every second spent on others is time we could have spent on the self, and any cent given to others is money that could have been spent on the self. We observe how our

7. Hovey, *To Share in the Body*, 60.

anxieties—our natural concerns over the well-being and preservation of the self—are heightened as the sacrifices grow larger and the impact upon the self becomes more keenly felt. In this we observe how the root dynamic— love in the face fear—is the same across the board, from the smallest acts of sacrifice to the largest acts of self-giving.

So let's turn to our third and final picture, again from Mr. Stringfellow, which will help illustrate the mundane nature of all this:

> How much or how often the churches are engaged in serving themselves instead of the world, that is, how far they have withdrawn from the ministry of the Body of Christ, are matters of practical consequence. For example, I had one day to fly to Boston to visit the Harvard Business School to give a lecture. I was late (some friends would say, as usual) in leaving my apartment to get out to the airport. Just as I was about to go, the telephone rang. I had not the will power not to answer it, in spite of my rush. It was a clergyman who was calling. "I have a woman in my office," he told me, "who is going to be evicted in the morning. Tell me what to do for her." I asked him a few questions and, it turned out, the grounds for the eviction were the non-payment of rent. The woman apparently had no money to pay her rent. She had, or asserted that she had, certain complaints against the landlord, but the complaints that she had were not sufficient, assuming that they could be legally established, to justify non-payment of the rent. They were no defense to the eviction, and if she wished to pursue them it would have to be done in a separate action against the landlord, apart from the eviction proceeding. By this time I was even more anxious about catching the airplane and said to the minister, "Well, sell one of your tapestries and pay the rent," and hung up and caught the plane. On the plane I thought the telephone conversation over and thought perhaps I had been rude and too abrupt in answering the minister that way and I considered calling him back after landing to apologize. But by the time the plane landed at Logan Airport I had rejected that idea. My answer had not been rude or irresponsible. On the contrary, exactly what he and the people of his congregation, which does have several beautiful and valuable tapestries, must be free to do is to sell their tapestries to pay the rent—to pay somebody else's rent—to pay anybody's rent who can't pay their own rent. If they have that freedom, then, but only then, does the tapestry have religious significance; only then does the tapestry enrich and contribute

to and express and represent the concern and care which Christians have in the name of God for the ordinary life of the world. The tapestry hanging in a church becomes and is a wholesome and holy thing, an appropriate and decent part of the scene of worship, only if the congregation which has the tapestry is free to take it down and sell it in order to feed the hungry or care for the sick or pay the rent or in any other way serve the world. The tapestry is an authentically Christian symbol only when it represents the freedom in Christ to give up any aspect of the inherited and present life of the institutional church, including, but not limited to, possessions, for the sake of the world.[8]

Notice Stringfellow's focus on freedom. The primary issue isn't whether or not the church *should* sell its tapestries to pay the woman's rent, as there are likely better ways to get the necessary money. Rather, the key issue for Stringfellow is the willingness to sell the tapestries, the *freedom* to make such a decision for the sake of the world. Recall our earlier discussions about McGill's notion of an identity of possession, an identity based on ownership. If the church treats its tapestries as possessions, then it must preserve and protect them against the claims of the world (like the individual who needed rent money to avoid eviction). In this instance, the church is not free to love, not free to undergo a loss or diminishment for the sake of others. Again, the issue isn't to decide whether selling tapestries is the best course of action, but rather to discover how the church forms its collective identity and whether the church is truly free to take sacrificial, loving action.

I like Stringfellow's story about tapestries as it removes the heroic frame we started with and illustrates the heart of the decisions we face every day—decisions about how we form our identities and how our identities inhibit or facilitate acts of love. The tapestries in Stringfellow's story represent those aspects of our lives that we are tempted to possess and defend in the face of the claims, demands, and needs of others. If anxiety over loss drives our hearts and minds, we will find it extraordinarily difficult to give away our "tapestries" for the sake of others.

3.

So now, with these pictures before us—from the Tibhirine monks, to Lou Marsh, to taking the last place in social settings, to church tapestries—let's turn to discuss concrete practices that help form identities able to love.

8. Stringfellow, *Private and Public Faith*, 78–79.

How are we to cultivate the freedom to give our lives away, in ways small and large?

To start, let's keep our focus on Arthur McGill's notion of an identity of possession. With this type of identity, we try to fend off death (with resources or with self-esteem) by controlling, owning, possessing, ruling over, and dominating some bit of reality. Basically, we become petty tyrants focused on protecting our homes, neighborhoods, reputations, statuses, nations, and egos from the needs and encroachments of others. In previous chapters we've noted how the great anxiety underneath this identity of possession—all this prickly and neurotic defending of our ego and turf—is a fear of loss and diminishment, a fear that someone will take something away from us. A fear of death.

When we've formed this sort of identity, how are we to become free in the ways described above? Free to live like the monks of Tibhirine or Lou Marsh? Free to take the last place? Free to "sell our tapestries" and make those small but very real sacrifices in our daily lives to give life to others? How are we to cultivate freedom from the anxiety that holds us back?

The answer, as described in chapters 5 and 6, is letting go of an identity of possession, dying to it, and adopting what David Kelsey calls an eccentric identity—an identity that is received from God and centered outside the self. The eccentric identity is experienced as *gift* rather than as *possession*.

So how do we come to experience this identity-as-gift? I like Kelsey's suggestion that the heart of the eccentric identity is *doxological gratitude*.[9]

Empirically speaking, this makes sense. Psychologists know that gratitude is one of the strongest predictors of happiness. To feel grateful is to experience life as a gift, as an experience of grace and joy. It's understandable, then, why gratitude—the experience of gift—would be the foundation of the eccentric identity.

But Kelsey goes beyond positive psychology. The type of gratitude he recommends is *doxological*   gratitude experienced as worship and expressed *within* worship.

This facet of the experience, the role of doxology, connects us back to our earlier discussions about basic and neurotic anxieties—the anxieties associated with survival and self-esteem. McGill's notion of an identity based on possession is predominately associated with basic anxiety and the attendant concerns over survival. That is, we tend to think of possessions as material resources that can be taken away from us, and we fear this loss. Thus, we can see how gratitude can function as a potent antidote for this sort of anxiety: if we view resources as gifts that are not our own, we are

---

9. See Kelsey, *Eccentric Existence*, 333–56.

much better positioned to share them with others. This dynamic—gratitude as antidote to anxiety—seems fairly straightforward. But our slavery to the fear of death also has neurotic manifestations. As we've noted, these neurotic anxieties are less fixated on issues of survival (the domain of basic anxiety) and more driven by the quest for self-esteem—the desire to appear significant in our eyes and the eyes of others. As we've described it, this pursuit is largely a game of trying to please, serve, and win the approbation of cultural institutions—the principalities and powers. This means that the identity of possession can be become as much *ego*-driven as *resource*-driven. If so, we need more than mere gratitude for material possessions to help break the anxious spell. That is, we tend to restrict gratitude to material blessings, but this restriction doesn't allow gratitude to infuse our self-concept and identity. We know what it feels like to be grateful for our house and income, but we don't tend to feel grateful for our reputation or for being perceived as witty, talented, or cool. We feel gratitude for *stuff*, but rarely for the *self*. We experience a Christmas sweater as a gift but less so our identities. Experiencing material things as gifts we can see how our gratitude would allow us to hold these things more lightly, enabling us to be more generous and open-handed with others. Gratitude promotes giving and letting go in this way. But do we feel that same gratitude about the self? *Are we willing to hold our self-esteem as lightly?* Or is the *self* a *possession* that must be protected? If we are willing to give material possessions away, are we also willing to let go of everything that makes us feel significant and worthy? Are we willing, in the words of Paul, to appear to be a "fool," perceived as "out of our mind" in the eyes of friends, family, coworkers, and the culture?

In short, mere gratitude—what we often find recommended within positive psychology self-help books—doesn't go deep enough. Though it is critical and necessary, simple thankfulness isn't sufficient to root out the anxious core of the self-esteem project, the way we become beholden to the principalities and powers or reliant upon our own talents, accomplishments, and abilities. In biblical language, mere gratitude doesn't address the *idolatry* inherent in our self-esteem projects. In fact, gratitude can become idolatrously misplaced. For example, we can start to feel grateful to and for *ourselves*. I feel grateful for myself being just so damn awesome.[10] And this is why gratitude must be *doxological* in nature, *an act of worship that exposes the self-esteem project as idolatry*, as a route toward self-glorification or as service to the principalities and powers. In this, doxological gratitude has

---

10. And I'd also add that a depressive self-esteem is simply the idolatrous inverse of this, the belief that your value, or lack thereof, is rooted in yourself.

a prophetic edge, calling into question and dismantling the death-driven ways our culture pursues meaning, significance, value, and self-esteem.

To summarize, key practices that form an eccentric identity are thanksgiving and worship. Doxological gratitude cultivates the experience of life as gift and prophetically rejects the idols of self-esteem enhancement proffered by the principalities and powers of the culture. Where *gratitude* combats the *basic anxieties* associated with the loss of resources, *worship* combats the *neurotic anxieties* associated with appearing "successful" in society's eyes. Consequently, it's not surprising that most of the New Testament's calls to ethical Christian living—which all boil down to the call to *love*—begin and end with expressions of *thanksgiving* and rounds of *praise* and doxology. The practices of doxological gratitude support a life of love. They create an eccentric identity, which in turn creates the capacity to give our lives away in acts of love for others. Hearts full of doxological gratitude are able to sell the tapestries, with joy and love, in small ways and large. Doxological gratitude helps us see that the tapestries were never ours to begin with. And this experience of gift makes sharing and taking the last place possible.

4.

Before moving on, let me say some concrete things about two specific practices of doxological gratitude.

First, any conversation about doxological gratitude and the practices of worship, thanksgiving, and prayer should pause to ponder the following sentiment, which is often attributed to Augustine: "The one who sings prays twice."

I believe it is significant that the prayer book of the Old Testament is a *songbook* and that in the New Testament Christians are commanded to sing. And yet, while I've heard many, many exhortations concerning the spiritual disciplines of prayer, fasting, silence, solitude, and simplicity, I've never heard *singing* mentioned (much less discussed) as a spiritual discipline. But I would argue that singing is, perhaps, one of the most important and fundamental of the spiritual disciplines, a key practice of cultivating an eccentric identity. As St. Paul exhorts:

> Be filled with the Spirit, speaking to one another with psalms, hymns, and songs from the Spirit. Sing and make music from your heart to the Lord, always giving thanks to God the Father for everything, in the name of our Lord Jesus Christ. (Eph 5:18b–20)

(margin handwritten note: Buddhist idea; There is no self.)

> Let the message of Christ dwell among you richly as you teach
> and admonish one another with all wisdom through psalms,
> hymns, and songs from the Spirit, singing to God with gratitude
> in your hearts. (Col 3:16)

As we see in Paul's exhortations, singing is a central practice of doxological gratitude. Singing is the practice of "giving thanks to God the Father
for everything." Singing is how we cultivate and express to God the "gratitude in [our] hearts." It is through singing that we most acutely come to
experience our lives as eccentrically grounded. It is through singing that
our expressions of gratitude become their most profound, reaching every
corner of heart and mind, body and soul. And it is through singing that we
learn to experience and receive our lives and identities as grace and gift.

And there is more to singing than expressing gratitude. Again, beyond
the experience of gift, doxological gratitude is also *prophetic* in nature as
worship calls into question the idols that would enslave us. Thus, as a practice of doxological gratitude, singing is also an act of resistance. Singing is as
much about *courage* as it is about gratitude. In this I'm reminded of Paul and
Silas singing in jail after being beaten and arrested in Philippi:

> The crowd joined in the attack against Paul and Silas, and the
> magistrates ordered them to be stripped and beaten with rods.
> After they had been severely flogged, they were thrown into
> prison, and the jailer was commanded to guard them carefully.
> When he received these orders, he put them in the inner cell and
> fastened their feet in the stocks.
>   About midnight Paul and Silas were praying and singing
> hymns to God, and the other prisoners were listening to them.
> (Acts 16:22–25)

The image is striking. Paul and Silas had just been savagely beaten. They had
open wounds, they were bruised and suffering from blood loss, and they
couldn't move much (even to relieve themselves) because their feet were in
stocks. They had to be feeling pretty grim and close to death.

And so they sang.

Why? They sang, as all fearful people do, to find and rekindle their
courage. I am put in mind here of how central and vital singing was to those
involved in the American civil rights movement. Singing is what drove the
movement. People would gather in churches and sing freedom songs before
going out to face angry mobs ready to curse at them, spit on them, even
violently beat them. And then, after they had been arrested, they would sing
on the way to jail. And then they sang *in* jail. These civil rights activists
never stopped singing. Why? For the same reason Paul and Silas sang. For

the same reason the early Christians sang in the catacombs. For the same reason we need to sing. To find our courage. Singing is a way of resisting despair and fear. Singing is an act of resistance.

I've witnessed this myself. I lead a weekly Bible study at a maximum-security prison. There are some nights when I can tell the men are down, depressed, discouraged, or despairing. They live in a brutal, dehumanizing place, and some weeks are hard weeks. And when I get the sense that it has been a particularly difficult week, before I get into my prepared material I have the men pass out the songbooks so that we can sing.

And once we start singing something starts to change. The singing gets better, louder. The mood becomes more hopeful. Spirits start to lift. Smiles start to appear. And once we start singing the men don't want to stop. They keep calling out numbers to hymns, and I keep my study notes tucked safely away. We sing on, into the night, just like Paul and Silas.

At root, the practices of doxological gratitude are practices aimed at battling fear. Singing is a practice of casting out fear. Singing is the exorcism of fear. Singing is the practice of creating, cultivating, and sustaining the courage we require to engage in acts of resistance as we face down the principalities and powers and—like Paul and Silas and those civil rights workers—even death itself.

5.

In addition to singing, let me also say something specific about the practice of prayer.

Nothing captures the posture of doxological gratitude—physically and spiritually—as well as prayer. If kenosis—letting go and emptying the self—is the concept, then prayer is the ritual, embodied enactment. In prayer we (quite literally) kneel and open our hands to God, eccentrically receiving from God our lives, identities, and everything we presume to "possess." Prayer is letting go, surrendering, opening up. Prayer is that posture—in action, word, or silence—where we do not possess anything but receive our lives as gift. The eccentric identity of Jesus is practiced and enacted when we open our hands and pray, as he prayed, "Father, into your hands I commit my spirit."

And as with singing there is more to prayer than surrendering and cultivating the experience of gift. Like all worship, prayer is also an act of prophetic resistance.

We see this twice in the book of Daniel, in which Shadrach, Meshach, and Abednego, and later Daniel himself, are persecuted for refusing to bow down or pray to the gods of Babylon. At root, prayer is an expression of allegiance. Prayer is a political act that calls into question the loyalties of the surrounding culture. In this, prayer becomes a critical practice of Christian renunciation, the cornerstone of the martyrological witness. This explains why prayer is the central weapon mentioned by Paul in his discussion in Ephesians 6 regarding our battle with the principalities and powers. For example, Walter Wink notes how politically provocative were the prayers of the early Christians in the face of imperial Rome:

> When the Roman *archons* (magistrates) ordered the early Christians to worship the imperial spirit or *genius*, they refused, kneeling instead and offering prayers on the emperor's behalf to God. This seemingly innocuous act was far more exasperating and revolutionary than outright rebellion would have been. Rebellion simply acknowledges the absoluteness and ultimacy of the emperor's power, and attempts to seize it. Prayer denies that ultimacy altogether by acknowledging a higher power. . . . [P]rayer challenged the very spirituality of the empire itself and called the empire's "angel," as it were, before the judgment seat of God.[11]

Here in this example of the early Christians we see how prayer aids in our fight against the principalities and powers. First, prayer denies the ultimacy of the powers, their claim to be divine, godlike and immune to death. Second, and perhaps most importantly, *prayer helps us resist internalizing the spirituality of the powers*. Like singing, prayer is a form of exorcism. In prayer the Angel of Death, the spirituality animating the powers, the spirituality that we are tempted to internalize as our own in our pursuit of a heroic identity, is renounced, rejected, and expelled.

6.

Above I've tried to show how the practices of doxological gratitude help us cultivate an eccentric identity, a Christ-shaped identity that creates a way of living that we've variously described as kenotic, cruciform, and martyrological. Such a life is characterized by the freedom to give our lives away. As Arthur McGill describes it:

> In Jesus Christ, therefore, we have the freedom to love; we have the freedom to love by laying down our life. The new kind of identity which Jesus brings involves this new life, a freedom

---

11. Wink, *Naming the Powers*, 110–11.

absolutely unthinkable to those who live by possession. The freedom to love is the freedom to do what Jesus did on the cross, the freedom to give ourselves away.[12]

And yet, having described all this, we now need to turn to a question that I have been putting off until this moment, an important objection to everything I have been encouraging.

Again, as we've described it, the relationship between fear and failures of love is shaped by the fact that love often involves a diminishment of the self. Fearing this diminishment, we become focused on self-preservation or the neurotic pursuit of self-esteem. We don't give our money, energy, or time to others because we fear we won't have enough for ourselves. We don't take the last place at the table because we fear being small, unnoticed, and insignificant in the face of death. We resist death, then, by inserting either resources or a heroic identity between ourselves and death. Both of these attempts produce sin: the buffer of resources makes us selfish and stingy, and the buffer of self-esteem makes us rivalrous, prideful, and violent: rivalrous toward in-group members doing better than we are; prideful toward in-group members doing worse than we are; and violent toward out-group members who question the values that support our heroic self-esteem project.

Obviously, selfish, envious, prideful, and violent people have a difficult time loving others because they are bound up by the psychological and behavioral expressions of a life enslaved to the fear of death. Resurrection, therefore, is a victory over this fear that results in the concrete expression of love toward others. Resurrection is the willingness to undergo a diminishment of the self and the ego in order to give life to others. Resurrection is perfect love casting out fear.

And yet, an objection might be raised at this point. Is this sort of life sustainable? We are limited and finite creatures. If love involves real loss and diminishment, is not the death of the self the logical outcome of this process? Metaphorically speaking, if our only transactions are withdrawals, it seems that the checks will eventually bounce. The self will become expended and used up. Surely this sort of existence cannot be sustained over time.

Can an isolated individual sustain this sort of lifestyle? At some point, as a consequence of our sacrificial giving, will not our situation and self become so diminished that we "givers" become the people in need? At what point along this continuum of diminishment and kenosis (emptying) should we stop and draw the line? When, if ever, do we establish boundaries

12. McGill, *Death and Life*, 76.

and set limits on the demands from others to provide for times of self-care, self-rehabilitation, and self-refreshment?

The Christian tradition provides no clear consensus on where these boundaries should be set, or if they should be set at all. Many individuals within the Christian tradition—people like St. Francis, Dorothy Day, and Mother Teresa come to mind—have set these boundaries in more "extreme" locations relative to the mass of Christians. Their heroic lives show the kenotic outcome of saying no to the self and yes to others more and more frequently, which supports the point made earlier that there is no radical or qualitative distinction between Christians in all this. There is simply a continuum of choices. There is always, in any given moment and decision, the possibility to move closer to love. Or further away. Thus, the act of Christian discipleship will always be a restless and open project. Every interaction we have with others places a demand upon us. As we make decisions in caring for others, we remain aware that there is always more that we might have done, more love we might have shown. For many Christians this open-endedness becomes difficult to bear. We begin to experience a lingering sense of guilt, of not doing enough since there is always more we can do. People manage these feelings in a variety of ways—some thirst for more "radical" forms of Christian expression, while others repress their pangs of guilt, wringing their hands for a moment but allowing the business (and busyness) of the day to carry them forward into forgetfulness.

There is much that could be said here about the importance of grace and the temptation to become driven by a works-based righteousness. For my part, in the face of these questions I return to the practices of doxological gratitude and use it as a diagnostic key. Joy and spontaneity are key indicators that love rather than guilt, shame, or fear is the engine of choice and sacrifice. Consequently, those of us struggling with shame, fear, guilt, or even spiritual competitiveness with others should stop and sit for a season with the practices of doxological gratitude. We should remain with worship and thanksgiving, singing and prayer, until joy, peace, and loving spontaneity return—fruits signaling that the eccentric identity of Jesus has been rehabilitated and restored in our hearts and minds. Yes, we can always do more, and people like St. Francis and Mother Teresa will always be out there as heroic exemplars. But any movement toward them—both the small and large steps—must be *infused with the joy that was exhibited in their own lives.* There will always be sacrifices to be made, but we should make them *only as far as our joy can carry us.* If we want to do *more,* that's alright, but the first work must be *joy,* the fruit of doxological gratitude. The renunciations of the cross are, at root, prompted by joy; thus we need to practice joy and allow it to carry us forward. With joy, we do not experience our sacrifices as grim burdens. In the words of Hebrews, we "fix our eyes on Jesus"—the "pioneer and perfecter of our faith"—who *"for the joy set before him* endured the cross." That's the key: we make sacrifices for the joy set before us.

7.

Having said this, I do think that questions about sustainability become a bit less acute if we shift our focus away from individuals and toward the community. To be blunt: we aren't asked to live this sacrificial life all by ourselves. God doesn't expect each of us to become a Christian version of Atlas (though many seem tempted by this messiah complex), holding up the whole world by our love and our efforts alone. Rather, God asks us to participate in communities that mutually practice sacrificial love. We love others while these same others love us in return. The issue of sustainability is only problematic when we think of love flowing in a single direction, out of ourselves and into others. If that's all that's occurring, then yes, we'll soon be empty. We'll be quickly used up. But if others are pouring back into us—if love is flowing in both directions—then we need not worry about our tanks running dry.

This is why Christian love is less about *sacrifice* than it is about *economy*, and why the experience of gift isn't *metaphorical* but *literal*. Something is indeed sacrificed in loving others—and with that comes a hurdle of fear to clear—but on the other side we find abundant life within the koinonia of the Kingdom. These are the dynamics that Jesus describes in Mark 10:

> As Jesus started on his way, a man ran up to him and fell on his knees before him. "Good teacher," he asked, "what must I do to inherit eternal life?"
>
> "Why do you call me good?" Jesus answered. "No one is good—except God alone. You know the commandments: 'You shall not murder, you shall not commit adultery, you shall not steal, you shall not give false testimony, you shall not defraud, honor your father and mother.'"
>
> "Teacher," he declared, "all these I have kept since I was a boy."
>
> Jesus looked at him and loved him. "One thing you lack," he said. "Go, sell everything you have and give to the poor, and you will have treasure in heaven. Then come, follow me."
>
> At this the man's face fell. He went away sad, because he had great wealth.
>
> Jesus looked around and said to his disciples, "How hard it is for the rich to enter the kingdom of God!"

The disciples were amazed at his words. But Jesus said again, "Children, how hard it is to enter the kingdom of God! It is easier for a camel to go through the eye of a needle than for someone who is rich to enter the kingdom of God."

The disciples were even more amazed, and said to each other, "Who then can be saved?"

Jesus looked at them and said, "With man this is impossible, but not with God; all things are possible with God."

Then Peter spoke up, "We have left everything to follow you!"

"Truly I tell you," Jesus replied, "no one who has left home or brothers or sisters or mother or father or children or fields for me and the gospel will fail to receive a hundred times as much in this present age: homes, brothers, sisters, mothers, children and fields—along with persecutions—and in the age to come eternal life. But many who are first will be last, and the last first." (Mark 10:17–31)

Jesus asks the rich young ruler to do something radical—to sell everything he owns and give it all to the poor. Not surprisingly, the young man succumbs to the fear of death. I know this not because I'm an amazing psychoanalyst. I know this because I can imagine what would be going through my mind if I were standing in this man's shoes. We are all familiar with the fear and anxiety this man was facing. It is slavery to the fear of death that holds us all back.

So it seems that Jesus is asking the man to make a *sacrifice*. In fact, in an attempt to gain Jesus' praise, Peter points to the sacrifices he and the others have made: "We have left everything to follow you!" But Jesus seems not to see it that way. According to Jesus, if the man is able to overcome his fear and lose his life there will be an abundance awaiting him in the life of the Kingdom. Jesus isn't asking the young man to give everything away and then starve to death as a beggar—to give to the point of his own death. Rather, Jesus is inviting the man to participate in the Jubilee of God's Kingdom economy. On the surface Jesus is asking the man to give away "everything," which is how Peter perceives the situation—that following Jesus is about loss and renunciation. Both Peter and the rich young ruler seem to think that following Jesus means losing everything. And it does—sort of. Because on the other side of the renunciation Jesus points to *social* (family and friends) and *material* (homes and fields) abundance. The sacrifice here isn't really about *material loss*. Rather, the sacrifice is one of *identity*, the loss of an identity formed by grasping and clinging. The sacrifice is about trust, and overcoming fear, and the eccentric existence of the Kingdom of

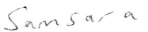

God—not *owning* homes and fields or friends and family, but instead *receiving these as gifts* in the loving economy of the Kingdom of God.

The Christian vision of love isn't the sacrificial heroism of the lone individual, for Jesus doesn't ask us to love the world all by ourselves. That's not sustainable. Rather, Jesus asks us to participate in *communities* of love, what he calls the Kingdom of God. Within these communities we undergo diminishment for the sake of others, but we are soon filled and rehabilitated by others. We sacrifice to find abundance waiting for us on the other side. That is the vision of church, as we read in Acts:

> All the believers were one in heart and mind. No one claimed that any of their possessions was their own, but they shared everything they had. With great power the apostles continued to testify to the resurrection of the Lord Jesus. And God's grace was so powerfully at work in them all that there were no needy persons among them. For from time to time those who owned land or houses sold them, brought the money from the sales and put it at the apostles' feet, and it was distributed to anyone who had need. (Acts 4:32–34)

We cannot deny that few churches truly look like this, but these communities do exist. In fact, many Christian groups are characterized by rich cultures of mutual aid, support, and sharing. Examples include monastic and intentional communities, new and old, as well as churches and small groups within churches that materially and emotionally assist each other during times of need. True, churches can be self-absorbed, image-driven, consumeristic institutions. But at their best church members rally to those in need, even if it's just showing up on the doorstep with a casserole. In these moments the church is living into the resurrection, drawing closer to the koinonia that Jesus envisions in Mark 10 and that characterized the early days of the Jesus movement.

As with individuals, churches also have choices to make about how much of themselves to give away for the sake of the world. And my goal here, as with our discussion above concerning individual choices, isn't to offer concrete recommendations for church life. Rather, my goal is to lay out how slavery to the fear of death becomes manifest in the face of such choices. To refer back to William Stringfellow's story, my concerns are less about the actual selling of the tapestries than about *the freedom of the church* to sell the tapestries. For it is this freedom that signals emancipation from slavery to the fear of death. It is this freedom that enables church communities to live for the sake of others.

8.

And yet, these communities are so difficult to form. Love cannot be manifested in the shared life of Christians until we become, again following Arthur McGill, a community of neediness.[13] The call is to participate in communities of self-giving love, and the prerequisite is the expression and sharing of our own needs. Notice in Acts 4 that there were "no needy persons among them." Why? Because they shared with "anyone one who had need." The expression of neediness in the community allowed the economy of love to flow. But in churches in America and other places where affluence poses special problems, the situation is very different. These cultures are enslaved to the fear of death and death avoidance holds serious sway. In these cultures the expression of need is taboo and pornographic. What results is neurotic image-management, the pressure to be "fine." The perversity here is that *on the surface American churches do look like the church in Acts 4*— there are "no needy persons" among us. We all appear to be doing just fine, thank you very much.

But we know this to be a sham, *a collective delusion driven by the fear of death*. I'm really not fine and neither are you. But you are afraid of me and I'm afraid of you. We are neurotic about being vulnerable with each other. We fear exposing our need and failure to each other. And because of this fear—the fear of being needy within a community of neediness—the witness of the church is compromised. A collection of self-sustaining and self-reliant people—people who are all pretending to be fine—is not the Kingdom of God. It's a church built upon the delusional anthropology we described earlier. Specifically, a church where everyone is "fine" is a group of humans *refusing to be human beings and pretending to be gods*. Such a "church" is comprised of fearful people working hard to keep up appearances and unable to trust each other to the point of loving self-sacrifice. In such a "church" each member is expected to be self-sufficient and self-sustaining, thus making no demands upon others. Unfortunately, where there is no need and no vulnerability, there can be no love.

So what is needed here are communal practices of vulnerability, confession, authenticity, and transparency—practices that enable us to share our needs and by which we are revealed, known and accepted as weak, needy, sinful, and broken. In all this, our slavery to the fear of death becomes very simple to understand. Love involves risk, and risk entails fear. Thus, love will always begin with an act of courage. And the courage needed here is of a particular sort—it is the courage to experience loss and diminishment,

---

13. McGill, *Death and Life*, 90.

to look like a fool or a failure, to express real need and give up being "fine" before others.

And when we are confronted with all this need, failure, and broken-ness, love will be the courage to listen to, accept, and care for each other. And love will be the courage to face down my fears that in caring for you I will be used up, wasted, poured out, and expended. Love will be the courage to trust that others will care for me as I care for you. Love will be trusting in the needy economy of love over the fear-driven temptation to be self-contained and self-sufficient, to retreat into being "fine" all by myself. And in stepping into this communal life we experience our liberation from slav-ery to the fear of death. In the Kingdom of God we experience love, life, and resurrection. In loving others and being loved in return, we move, in the words of St. John, "from death to life" (1 John 3:14 NIV).

9.

Still, the fears here are acute and hard to overcome in one gigantic step. And all this talk about martyrdom and radical self-expenditure can seem a bit much, overly dramatic for people with day jobs. So let me conclude with one more spiritual practice, something modest that I think we can all begin with, something small in execution but radical in ambition. A way of "giving your life way" that everyone can aspire to. Even people with day jobs.

The practice I mean is "the Little Way" of St. Thérèse of Lisieux.

10.

On the surface, the story of Thérèse is a curious one. Thérèse Martin was born on January 2, 1873, in Alençon, France. Her parents were two very devout Catholics, Louis and Zelie Martin. The family had a very high view of monastic life, as both parents tried in their early lives to join a monastic community. Eventually, two of Thérèse's older sisters—Pauline and Marie—entered the cloistered Carmelite monastery in Lisieux, Normandy.

Thérèse herself was spiritually precocious and wanted to follow her sisters into the Carmelite community. But she chafed at having to wait until she was sixteen years of age. She eventually petitioned Pope Leo XIII for a special dispensation to enter the monastery early. This was granted and on April 9, 1888, at the age of fifteen, Thérèse joined her sisters at Carmel.

From all external perspectives Thérèse's years at Carmel were quiet and uneventful. She dutifully participated in the life of the community, but without outward distinction. She did love to write, often composing plays to be put on by the sisters.

In the early morning hours of Good Friday in 1896 Thérèse awoke to find her mouth filled with blood. After a painful struggle with tuberculosis for well over a year Thérèse died, after two days of great pain, on September 30, 1897. She was twenty-four.

Here's where the story gets interesting. In 1925, a mere twenty-eight years after her death, Pope Pius XI presided over Thérèse's sainthood. And since her death Thérèse has become one of the most popular Catholic saints. Moreover, in 1997 Pope John Paul II named Thérèse a doctor of the church, thus making her a saint among the saints, in the company of theologians such as Augustine and Aquinas. Only three women are doctors of the church—Teresa of Avila, Catherine of Siena, and Thérèse of Lisieux.

What is interesting about all this is the contrast between the quietness of Thérèse's life and the accolades that so quickly followed her death—worldwide devotion, sainthood, becoming a doctor of the church. No miracles were associated with Thérèse during her lifetime. She never left Carmel. She started no new monastic orders. She did nothing, externally, that drew attention. She was just one nun among other nuns in a cloistered community. And even among her fellow sisters Thérèse's life was unremarkable. In fact, when Thérèse died, one of her fellow sisters worried that no one would have anything to say at Thérèse's funeral! Never was a saint more unnoticed. And remember, Thérèse died when she was twenty-four. What could such a young person have to say to make her a doctor of the church?

The impact of Thérèse rests upon the influence of her spiritual memoir, *Histoire d'une Ame* (*Story of a Soul*).

Story of a Soul was published the year after Thérèse's death in 1898. And much to the surprise of her fellow Carmelite sisters, it gained widespread notoriety and influence. During her lifetime, few around Thérèse sensed that a spiritual hurricane raged inside of her, that her quiet and humble exterior hid one of the great spiritual teachers of the modern age. Who knew that spiritual greatness could be so quiet, bland, and normal looking?

This is why I think the spirituality and story of Thérèse is important for our purposes. The life of Thérèse suggests that the call to give our lives away might be realized in fairly mundane circumstances. Thérèse teaches us that we've become confused about what sainthood and heroic discipleship might look like. In following Jesus we often picture something grand and headline-grabbing. But the life of Thérèse suggests that sainthood can be quiet and nondescript. One of the greatest of saints—a doctor of the church, even, on par with Augustine and Aquinas—can be the person checking you out at Walmart, or the old lady sitting by you at church, or the mom with two toddlers, or the college student, or the janitor taking out the trash in your office.

In short, if at any point here in Part 3—with all my talk of martyrs, self-expenditure, and giving your life away—I have left you with the impression that the way of Jesus is too huge, ambitious, heroic, and radical for you to reach, I'd like to end our discussion of practices with the path Thérèse set before us.

Which is to say, don't despair. I really think you can do this.

11.

Thérèse's spiritual memoir, *Story of a Soul*, became a sensation. As noted, it led to worldwide devotion, culminating in Thérèse's sainthood in 1925. But it was the theological content of *Story of a Soul*, with its discussion of the spirituality of the Little Way, that led to Thérèse's becoming a doctor of the church in 1997. Students of the Little Way include such spiritual luminaries as Dorothy Day, Thomas Merton, and Mother Teresa.

So, what is the Little Way?

Wanting to live a radical life of self-expenditure, Thérèse dreamed of living a heroic life like her countrywoman Joan of Arc. She wanted to die a martyr on a foreign mission field. But instead, Thérèse found herself in a cloistered monastic community that, given the rigid structures of life there, offered few heroic opportunities for advancing the cause of Christ. Life consisted of daily chores and duties and getting along with the sisters she was living with. I expect most of us can identify. How are we going to express our emancipation from our slavery to death in radical self-expenditure for others? We have bills to pay, a lawn to mow, kids to pick up, a boss to please.

Feeling hemmed in and limited in her options, Thérèse began to search for alternative ways, more modest ways, to make sacrifices in love for others. What she found was not a heroic path, but a little way—a way that consisted of making small, seemingly insignificant sacrifices in loving others. The Little Way involves small acts of daily relinquishment: acts of humility, restraint, self-control, forbearance, perseverance, patience, and long-suffering. The Little Way is about "bearing with" people. The dying to self here is less about heroic martyrdom than it is about holding your tongue, refusing to gossip, waiting patiently, mastering your irritation, avoiding the spotlight, refusing to respond to insults, allowing others to cut in line, being first to apologize, and not seeking to win every argument. The Little Way is about mastering the many daily eruptions of neurotic anxiety, anger, vanity, and envy that routinely interrupt our ability to extend grace, love, and kindness to others.

But most importantly, the Little Way is the active pursuit of loving others. To give some concrete examples, in the final chapter of *Story of a Soul*, Thérèse describes her own practice of the Little Way:

> I have noticed (and this is very natural) that the most saintly Sisters are the most loved. We seek their company; we render them services without their asking; finally, these souls so capable of bearing the lack of respect and consideration of others see themselves surrounded with everyone's affection. . . .
>
> On the other hand, imperfect souls are not sought out. No doubt we remain within the limits of religious politeness in their regard, but we generally avoid them, fearing lest we say something which isn't too amiable. When I speak of imperfect souls, I don't want to speak of spiritual imperfections since most holy souls will be perfect in heaven; but I want to speak of a lack of judgment, good manners, touchiness in certain characters; all these things which don't make life agreeable. I know very well that these moral infirmities are chronic, that there is no hope of a cure, but I also know that my Mother would not cease to take care of me, to try to console me, if I remained sick all my life. This is the conclusion I draw from this: I must seek out in recreation, on free days, the company of Sisters who are the least agreeable to me in order to carry out with regard to these wounded souls the office of the Good Samaritan. A word, an amiable smile, often suffice to make a sad soul bloom. . . .[14]

As I am sure is the case in your own social sphere, workplace, church, and extended family, Thérèse was surround by two sorts of people. On the one hand were the well-adjusted and the popular; on the other hand were the "imperfect souls," the people who were, to borrow Thérèse's descriptions, ill-mannered, touchy, and lacking in judgment. You may know such people— the irritating, annoying, and crabby ones who "don't make life agreeable." The faults named here are characterological in nature. As Thérèse notes, there is no hope of a cure for these individuals. They are chronically, albeit socially, sick.

And yet, Thérèse goes on, would not a mother care for her sick child?

The answer is yes. And so love draws Thérèse to actively seek out these damaged and annoying individuals and to spend time with them. She offers smiles and kind words. And she calls these small acts "the office of the Good Samaritan"—showing care to a wounded person. These are little

---

14. Thérèse of Lisieux, *Story of a Soul*, 245–46.

things, modest acts of self-giving, self-sacrifice, and self-expenditure. Still, we tend to think of the Good Samaritan in heroic terms. But if you consider the damaged and irritating people in your own life—please bring them to mind right now—and then ponder *actively seeking these people out* in order to show some kindness, affection, and care, you'll quickly realize just how radical—and damn near heroic—is the practice of the Little Way.

Consider one more example. When we think of Jesus's radical command to love our enemies, we often jump, again, to the heroic vision of nonviolent self-sacrifice. This is the martyrological ideal that scares us, as it might have scared you when I first mentioned it, when we hear the word *martyr*. But your life is probably a lot like Thérèse's at Carmel. Odds are you aren't surrounded by bloodthirsty enemies wanting to burn you at the stake. So what does it mean to "love your enemies" in those circumstances? Thérèse describes her Little Way of loving enemies:

> The Lord, in the Gospel, explains in what His new command-ment consists. He says in St. Matthew: *"You have heard that it was said, 'You shall love your neighbor and hate your enemy.' But I say to you, love your enemies . . . pray for those who persecute you."* No doubt, we don't have any enemies in Carmel, but there are feelings. One feels attracted to this Sister, whereas with re-gard to another, one would make a long detour in order to avoid meeting her. And so, without knowing it, she becomes the sub-ject of persecution. Well, Jesus is telling me that it is this Sister who must be loved. . . .[15]

Again, I'm sure you can identify with Thérèse. While we might not have proper enemies, there are "feelings." And these "feelings" we have toward some people—often legitimately so—cause us to be repelled by them. Again, we can all bring to mind a person who is universally repellant and so is collectively avoided. Haven't you, as Thérèse mentions, made long detours around people in order to avoid them? Shoot, I detour around people at *church*.

What is remarkable is how Thérèse calls this social stigmatization and avoidance—our long detouring around people—a form of *persecution*. And as Thérèse unpacks it, loving our enemies means dismantling these social barriers, refusing to take those detours, and welcoming and including these individuals. The Little Way is engaging in small acts of hospitality. And again, while establishing a "no-detour rule" for yourself might seem to be a little thing, it is, upon considered reflection, a pretty monumental and life-changing step to take.

15. Ibid., 224–25

And yet, it's such a small thing. Little acts of welcome and hospitality demand no huge outlay of time or resources. The sacrifices here are largely internal, giving up things we'd prefer, things we find pleasing or rewarding, in order to step in the name of love into experiences that we wouldn't normally choose, be attracted to, or find intrinsically rewarding. And yet, this "Little Way," while seemingly small on the surface, hides beneath it a truly heroic form of self-giving and self-sacrifice. And if the lives of Thérèse's followers, including Dorothy Day and Mother Teresa, are any evidence, these small acts of self-giving and self-expenditure can add up in impressive ways.

But this is a practice of love that starts on a small scale and builds by slow, imperceptible, daily accretion. It begins, simply, with a smile. With a kind word. With an invitation to coffee. With a small act of inclusion, welcome, and hospitality. With no more detours.

Chapter 8

The Freedom of God

1.

Having envisioned life set free from our slavery to the fear of death and practices that can cultivate and sustain such a life, we must deal with one final issue: the slavery of God.

2.

In Part 2, when we wrestled with the work of Ernest Becker, we analyzed how cultural hero systems function as neurotic defense mechanisms that help us deal with our sense of meaninglessness and futility in the face of death. Consequently, when we participate in these hero systems—usually by serving the principalities and powers—our self-identity and self-esteem become enslaved to the fear of death. Fearing death—neurotically manifested as a fear of "failure" or being needy in American culture—we slavishly pursue "success" as it is defined by the surrounding culture. Even more troubling, we become hostile toward out-group members who call our hero system into question.

The great problem in all this—a problem we need to face before concluding—is how God and religion undergird and support the cultural hero system. Cultural hero systems and religion are deeply interconnected—in fact, they are generally synonymous—with our "God" or "gods" providing the warrant for our way of life. Recall that in order for hero systems to confer immunity in the face of death, they must be experienced as immortal and eternal. And there is no better way to create that sense of immortality than to baptize and sacralize the hero system, to fuse our way of life with the way of God.

What this means is that "God" and religious institutions can become as enslaved to the fear of death as everything else in the culture. The church can become as much a principality and power as any other cultural institution. And if this is so, service to "God" and "the church" can produce satanic outcomes as much as, if not more so, any other form of service to the power of death in our world.

In biblical terms, this is idolatry—when "God" and religion become another form of our slavery to the fear of death, another fallen principality and power demanding slavish service and loyalty. Idolatry is when our allegiances to the faith-based principalities and powers, and the cultural institutions they are wedded to (e.g., the nation-state), keep us enslaved to death, bound to the fear-driven cycle of sin as we become paranoid and hostile toward out-group members. It's not news that much of the hostility and violence in the world has been rooted in religious conflict.

Idolatry, then, is *the slavery of God* where "God" and "the church" become another manifestation of our slavery to death, another form of "the devil's work" in our lives.

3.

So how are we to be set free from this idolatry? How are we to proclaim and experience the freedom of God?

In the Old Testament, the battle with idolatry was fought by the prophets. And at its heart, the prophetic impulse is to proclaim the emancipation of God, the freedom of God, the liberty of God. The ambition of the prophet is to end the slavery of God.

That might seem counterintuitive, as we tend to think of the prophets as proclaiming liberty and emancipation to human beings in bondage. The prototype of all prophetic utterance in the life of Israel was Moses's proclaiming "Let my people go!" before Pharaoh. But before such a proclamation can be made—before the prophetic cry of "Let justice roll down like a river!"—something more fundamental has to take place. For the prophet, before freedom is proclaimed to the *slaves,* the freedom of *God* must be pronounced. God is the first slave set free by the prophet, and in the wake of that liberation the liberation of all other slaves will follow.

Walter Brueggemann makes this argument in his book *The Prophetic Imagination.* According to Brueggemann, the primal taproot of all prophetic utterance was the declaration of Moses that YHWH was *free*—free enough to be *against* Pharaoh. This proclamation of "againstness" is the wellspring of all prophetic judgment. The prophet proclaims that God cannot be identified with the status quo—however shiny, powerful, immortal, or divine that status quo may appear. The principalities and powers will always seek to capture and enslave God in an attempt to use the name of God to underwrite current power arrangements. To go against the status quo, declare the powers, is to go against God. Religion in this instance becomes another fear-based cudgel, wielded to protect the interests of the principalities and powers and those who currently benefit from business as usual, thus aiding in their success and survival. Consequently, before proclamation to human captives can be made—freedom to those being oppressed by current power arrangements—the prophet must dare to proclaim that God is not the spokesperson for the status quo, but rather stands *outside* the system—free—to speak a word of judgment. When the freedom of God is proclaimed, when God is outside the system and free to bring a word of indictment against us, the capacity is created to speak on behalf of the marginalized and the disfranchised *in the name of God*. Being free, God can now be for the weak and the least of these over against those at the top of current power arrangements. This was the real shock at the heart of Moses's prophetic utterance to Pharaoh—*that God was on the side of the slaves and stood with them over against the divinely ordained power and authority of Egypt*. As Brueggemann writes:

> In place of the gods of Egypt, creatures of the imperial consciousness, Moses discloses that Yahweh, the sovereign one who acts in his lordly freedom, is extrapolated from no social reality and is captive to no social perception but acts from his own person toward his own purposes.[1]

This proclamation—that God cannot be extrapolated from nor identified with current "social reality," that God does not underwrite current power arrangements—is the prerequisite for the proclamation of emancipation on behalf of human beings currently enslaved, exploited, ignored, and pushed to the margins of society. Brueggemann here makes the connection:

> We will not have a politics of justice and compassion unless we have a religion of God's freedom. We are indeed made in the image of some God. And perhaps we have no more important theological investigation than to discern in whose image we have been made. . . . [I]f we gather around a static god of order

---

1. Brueggemann, *Prophetic Imagination*, 6.

who only guards the interests of the "haves," oppression cannot be far behind. Conversely, if a God is disclosed who is free to come and go, free from and even against the regime, free to hear and even answer slave cries, free from all proper goodness as defined by the empire, then it will bear decisively upon sociology because the freedom of God will surface in the brickyards and manifest itself as justice and compassion.[2]

God must be set free, and remain so radically free that God can speak a word of judgment against us on behalf of those we oppress.

4.

This capacity for prophetic imagination, that God is free to be against us, is the great weapon against idolatry. Whenever and wherever the people of God lose this capacity, God becomes enslaved. When the prophetic imagination is eclipsed—when God can no longer be imagined as being *against us* and *for those* we oppress, exclude, stigmatize, marginalize, ignore, or aggress against—God is no longer free but a slave. In that event, with the silencing of the prophetic voice within the faith community (or those voices of critique from the outside), God is no longer God but a principality and power—a tool of the devil—leading us into sin.

And what might be the sign of this eclipse of the prophetic voice? What are the symptoms of this failure of the prophetic imagination? Simply put, *the alignment of, equating of, and identification of our voice and interests with God's own.* This occurs when we speak for God with no remainder, when we see ourselves as God's favored ones engaged in holy crusades, and when the current power arrangements are legitimized as being ordained or endorsed by God. In these instances God has been captured, and the demonic dynamics of our slavery to death are soon set into motion. Dogmatism, triumphalism, and exceptionalism are clear attitudinal indicators here. But the clearest behavioral sign is the failure of kenosis with the onset—in the name of God!—of grasping, protecting, and aggressing rather than emptying, serving and giving.

5.

Phrased in the language we have been using in this book, the prophet proclaims the eccentric nature of God. God is not a *possession* of the faith

2. Ibid., 7–8

community—a possession that, like all possessions, can be lost or damaged and that requires protecting or defending. God is experienced eccentrically, as coming to us from *outside the boundaries of the faith community*. God is not owned by an individual or by the church, the nation, or any other human institution. God is not a possession of any person or community. God is always free, beyond our borders and boundaries. This eccentricity is the source of God's freedom. When eccentrically experienced God cannot be owned, captured, or possessed by the faith community.

In more conventional terms the experience of the eccentric God is the experience of grace and gift. Grace is the gratuitous movement of God toward us from beyond our boundaries, from the "outside," as it were. In this we see how the freedom of God is both the source of prophetic utterance as well as the source of grace. Here we return once more to the experience of doxological gratitude.

As we described in the last chapter, the worship of God—doxology—is a prophetic act, the recognition that God alone is Sovereign, Lord over all powers. In our earlier discussions we noted how in worship, baptism, and the daily taking up of the cross there is a renunciation of our prior allegiances to the principalities and powers. But what we are wrestling with here is this: what if *God* has become the principality and power? What if *God* has become the idol, the manifestation of our slavery to the fear of death? What are we to do in that instance?

The deep and hard insight here is that, if God has been enslaved, then God must stand over and against our current conceptions of "God," over and against the idols we believe to be "God." In worship God must be free to stand over "God," the fear-based idols we have created to validate our cultural way of life, the blue ribbons of our self-esteem projects, and our stigmatization of out-group members. This is a worship so profound, a worship so deep and destabilizing, that it can stand in judgment of our worship. *This is the capacity for a worship that can admit that God despises our worship.* A worship in which God is free to speak, as did the prophets, an indictment against our worship and religion: "I hate, I despise your religious feasts; I cannot stand your assemblies" (Amos 5:21 NIV). When this capacity exists—when God is free to be against the cultural idols called "God"—the freedom of God is decisively manifest and the prophetic imagination fully realized.

This is how we know that God has been emancipated and set free from our slavery to the fear of death: *When we can hear the voice of God crying out against us in the voices of those we ignore, marginalize, victimize, exclude, ostracize, harm, and kill, we know that God has been set free.* The radical, prophetic freedom of God is fully realized when we see the face of God in our victims and our enemies. In that moment our slavery to the fear of death is fully overcome. In that moment the sacrificial love of Christ becomes fully manifest.

In that moment the Kingdom comes, on earth as it is in heaven.

Epilogue

The Harrowing of Hell

1.

It's Easter and I'm looking at the icon on my wall.

In the Western Christian tradition, particularly among Protestants, the dominant image on Easter Sunday is a picture of an empty tomb. We don't see Jesus anywhere in that picture. Rather, we see morning sunlight, a rocky hillside, a gaping hole, and a large circular rock rolled to the side. That's not the icon I'm looking at.

In the icon I'm looking at I see Jesus standing in the middle of the scene. He's reaching out and holding the hands of two old people—an old man and an old woman. And there is a great crowd of people standing behind them.

The scene looks to be underground. There are smashed gates on the ground. Keys are on the floor. And a dark figure is being bound by angels.

What I'm looking at is the Easter icon of the Orthodox Church. It's a depiction of what is known as the harrowing of hell.

2.

The harrowing of hell is an obscure doctrine in the West. Moreover, it's becoming increasingly scandalous with certain Protestant Christians. I recently took note of some evangelical church leaders who were wondering if a phrase like "He descended into hell" should be dropped from confessional statements such as the Apostles' Creed. Many Protestant Christians seem to be at a loss with the Christus Victor themes of the Bible.

Regardless, there is biblical evidence for the harrowing of hell, the belief that after his death Jesus descended into hell to free captive humanity, to liberate those held by Satan in bondage to death:

> For Christ died for sins once for all, the righteous for the unrighteous, to bring you to God. He was put to death in the body but made alive by the Spirit, through whom also *he went and preached to the spirits in prison who disobeyed long ago.* . . . (1 Pet 3:18–20a; my italics)

> This is why it says:
>   "When he ascended on high,
>   *he led captives in his train*
>   and gave gifts to men."
> (What does "he ascended" mean except that *he also descended to the lower, earthly regions?* He who descended is the very one who ascended higher than all the heavens, in order to fill the whole universe.)
> (Eph 4:8–10; my italics)

This belief that Christ descended into hell after his death is also captured in Peter's Pentecost sermon in Acts 2:

> . . . because you will not abandon me to *the realm of the dead,* you will not let your holy one see decay. (Acts 2:27)

These are some of the texts that informed the Christus Victor theology of the early church, the theological vision that has informed this book—the belief that salvation is, at root, a liberation and emancipation from the slavery of death. An emancipation that also sets us free from the power of the devil.

In this book I've approached these themes from a distinctly modern and psychological perspective. But in the depiction of the harrowing of hell I see an artistic representation of the root idea that we started with and carried through the pages of this book. The icon in front of me is a visual representation of the Orthodox notion that our fundamental predicament is less about sin than it is about death, and that the fear of death is the tool of Satan in our lives. In the harrowing of hell icon I'm reminded that the work of Christ is to free us from the power of death and to destroy the works of the devil. To that I say, Amen and Amen.

So this Easter, as I look at the icon of the harrowing of hell, I'm thinking of resurrection. It is Easter, after all. And the vision before me isn't the traditional view of the open tomb. Rather, in the icon in front of me I'm seeing myself in that deep cave of death, along with Adam and Eve—the two old people reaching out to Jesus in the icon—and all the rest of captive humanity. On Resurrection Sunday I'm thinking of Christ setting us free from our slavery to death, which has held us captive, in the words of Hebrews, all our lives.

And as I see Satan being bound—he's the dark figure in the icon being held by angels—the words from that old, old sermon by John Chrysostom drift back to me: "He who does not fear death is outside the tyranny of the devil."

And the words of St. John soon follow, saying everything that I've tried to share with you:

> We know that we have left death and come over into life;
> we know it because we love others (1 John 3:14 GNB).

Acknowledgments

I remember well, in graduate school, stumbling upon a copy of Ernest Becker's *The Denial of Death* in a used bookstore. What I found within its covers stunned and shook me. I knew I had found something that required, even demanded of me, a spiritual and theological reckoning. So began a very long spiritual and intellectual journey.

In the years and decades following my encounter with Becker's seminal work in existential psychology, I was on a constant hunt for theological perspectives that could help me put the pieces together. After many years of searching, I finally found my guides in the theological work in William Stringfellow and Arthur McGill. Here were two theologians who placed the predicament of death at the center of their theological reflections. If you read Becker, Stringfellow, and McGill side by side, you'll notice remarkable convergences. This became the bridge that helped me connect psychology and theology in forming some answers to the questions posed by *The Denial of Death*.

And yet, the existential perspectives of Becker, Stringfellow, and McGill can seem very modern and disconnected from the world of the early church and the biblical text. The final piece of the puzzle snapped into place when I encountered Orthodox theology. Here was, in its Christus Victor orientation and notion of ancestral (rather than original) sin, a theological paradigm that also placed death at the center of our predicament but that was also very old and connected to the earliest church fathers.

All these pieces culminated in the mix you find on the pages of this book: a fusion of existential psychology (Becker), modern theology (Stringfellow, McGill), and early patristic thought (Orthodoxy theology). I hope the synthesis I have attempted here prompts continued interdisciplinary reflection and conversation.

I would like to extend my deep gratitude to the readers of my blog, *Experimental Theology*. My daily interactions with each of you have been a source of deep spiritual encouragement and constant intellectual stimulation. You were the ones who encouraged me to pull this material into book form, and your comments helped shape and direct the final product. I hope the book blesses you and you feel a sense of ownership as you hold it.

Thanks once again to the great team at Wipf and Stock for producing another beautiful book. A special thanks to Charlie Collier, who pointed me to the issue of *timor mortis* in the thought of Augustine.

I'd also like to express appreciation for the work of David Kelsey for two terms and related concepts—eccentric identity and doxological gratitude—that I hope I put to good use in the book.

Walter Wink passed away in 2012, the year in which this book was written. Obviously, I and many others lean heavily upon his seminal work regarding the principalities and powers. Much gratitude for his work, his life, and his witness for peace.

Let me also express my deep appreciation to Anne Briggs for her encouragement, her friendship, and for all her editorial help.

As always, I'm so grateful for my family:

Brenden and Aidan, you are my joy. I hope you read this book when you grow up. It contains your father's best take on what it means for us to take up our cross and follow Jesus.

As for my wife, readers should know that everything I think and write gets its first hearing with Jana. Jana is the other heart and mind behind these pages.

Jana, you are the love of my life. TIL.

Finally, I've dedicated this book to my mother and father, Richard and Paula Beck. I wrote most of this book during the annual Beck family beach vacation in the summer of 2012, sitting at Mom and Dad's breakfast table. A great theme of this book is how love is a form of emptying in order to give life to others. Mom and Dad, over and over you've emptied yourself to give life to me. And for that, I'm eternally grateful.

Richard Beck
Advent 2012

Bibliography

Augustine. *Concerning the City of God against the Pagans.* Translated by Henry Bettenson. New York: Penguin, 2003.

Aulén, Gustaf. *Christus Victor: An Historical Study of the Three Main Types of the Idea of Atonement.* Translated by A. G. Hebert. 1951. Reprint, Eugene, OR: Wipf & Stock, 2003.

Baumeister, Roy. *Evil: Inside Human Violence and Cruelty.* New York: Henry Holt, 1999.

Becker, Ernest. *The Denial of Death.* New York: Simon & Schuster, 1973.

————. *Escape from Evil.* New York: Free Press, 1975.

Bonhoeffer, Dietrich. *The Cost of Discipleship.* New York: Simon and Schuster, 1995.

Brueggemann, Walter. *The Message of the Psalms: A Theological Commentary.* Minneapolis: Augsburg Fortress, 1984.

————. *The Prophetic Imagination.* 2nd ed. Minneapolis: Augsburg Fortress, 2001.

Dodaro, Robert. *Christ and the Just Society in the Thought of Augustine.* New York: Cambridge University Press, 2004.

Dunn, James. *The Theology of Paul the Apostle.* Grand Rapids: Eerdmans, 1998.

Episcopal Church. *The Book of Common Prayer.* New York: Seabury, 1979.

Gorer, Geoffrey. *Death, Grief, and Mourning.* Garden City, NY: Anchor, 1967.

Hauerwas, Stanley. *Working With Words: On Learning to Speak Christian.* Eugene, OR: Cascade, 2011.

Heim, S. Mark. *The Depth of the Riches: A Trinitarian Theology of Religious Ends.* Grand Rapids: Eerdmans, 2001.

Hovey, Craig. *To Share in the Body: A Theology of Martyrdom for Today's Church.* Grand Rapids: Brazos, 2008.

Kelsey, David H. *Eccentric Existence: A Theological Anthropology.* Vol 1. Louisville: Westminster John Knox, 2009.

Kiser, John. *The Monks of Tibhirine: Faith, Love, and Terror in Algeria.* New York: St. Martin's Griffin, 2003.

Lilla, Mark. *The Stillborn God.* New York: Knopf, 2007.

McGill, Arthur C. *Death and Life: An American Theology.* Edited by Charles A. Wilson and Per M. Anderson. 1987. Reprint, Eugene, OR: Wipf and Stock, 2003.

Of Gods and Men. Directed by Xavier Beauvois. 2010. Prague, Czech Republic: Armada Films and Why Not Productions. DVD.

Romanides, John S. *The Ancestral Sin.* Ridgewood, NJ: Zephyr, 2002

Solomon, Sheldon, Jeff Greenberg, and Tom Pyszczynski. "The Cultural Animal: Twenty Years of Terror Management Theory and Research." In *Handbook of*

Experimental Existential Psychology, edited by Jeff Greenberg, Sander L. Koole, and Tom Pyszczynski, 13–34. New York: Guilford, 2004.

Straw, Carole. "*Timor Mortis.*" In *Augustine Through the Ages: An Encyclopedia*, edited by Allan Fitzgerald et al., 838–42. Grand Rapids: Eerdmans, 1999.

Stringfellow, William. *An Ethic for Christians and Other Aliens in a Strange Land.* 1973. Reprint, Eugene, OR: Wipf & Stock, 2004.

———. *Free in Obedience.* 1964. Reprint, Eugene, OR: Wipf & Stock, 2006.

———. *Instead of Death.* 1976. Reprint, Eugene, OR: Wipf & Stock, 2004.

———. *My People Is the Enemy: An Autobiographical Polemic.* 1964. Reprint, Eugene, OR: Wipf & Stock, 2005.

———. *A Private and Public Faith.* 1962. Reprint, Eugene, OR: Wipf & Stock, 1999.

———. *A Simplicity of Faith: My Experience in Mourning.* 1979. Reprint, Eugene, OR: Wipf & Stock, 2005.

Thérèse of Lisieux. *Story of a Soul: The Autobiography of St. Thérèse of Lisieux.* Translated by John Clarke. 3rd ed. Washington, DC: ICS, 1996.

Thurman, Howard. *Jesus and the Disinherited.* Boston: Beacon, 1976.

Vanier, Jean. *Community and Growth.* Rev. ed. New York: Paulist, 1989.

Wink, Walter. *Engaging the Powers.* Minneapolis: Fortress, 1992.

———. *Naming the Powers.* Philadelphia: Fortress, 1984.

———. *Unmasking the Powers.* Philadelphia: Fortress, 1986.

Wright, N. T. *Simply Jesus.* New York: HarperCollins, 2011.